Mountain Stallion

Logan Forster

Mountain Stallion

Books by Logan Forster

PROUD LAND

DESERT STORM

MOUNTAIN STALLION

MOUNTAIN STALLION

LOGAN FORSTER

Illustrated by Jessie Forster

DODD, MEAD & COMPANY • NEW YORK • 1958

Library of Congress Catalog Card Number: 56-5489

Printed in the United States of America
by The Haddon Craftsmen, Inc., Scranton, Penna.

ʌʌʌʌʌʌ

Contents

Mountain Stallion

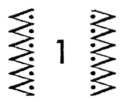 1

Return to Glory

PONCE sat motionless on the bench in the jockeys' room, his dark eyes fixed on the floor between his booted feet. Only one accustomed to reading Indian faces could have detected the signs of tension beneath the still features, and only one who knew him personally could have known of the nervousness and breathlessness gripping him. He seemed utterly unconcerned there in the middle of the crowded room where some fifty riders milled, shouted, laughed and discussed the past races and those yet to be run.

Absently he reached up and smoothed the black mane of hair that hung below his shoulders. Instantly he wished he could recall the gesture, as a half dozen pairs of eyes swung on him and settled. "Don't let it bother you," he told himself angrily. "You wear it thus, because you want them all to know that you are an Apache and proud of your people. Don't worry about what they are thinking."

A voice came from his left. "You're the fellow called Ponce who owns the big black filly, aren't you?"

He turned and looked into a pair of blue eyes that reminded him of the deep, cloudless skies of his native Arizona. He stared hard at those eyes, and at the face that had the starved look peculiar to jockeys the world over. There was no rude

1

curiosity, no laughter, no sarcasm. The young man seemed to be genuinely interested in him.

"Yes," Ponce murmured. "That is right."

The other nodded, smiling. "I've seen you around quite a bit lately. Just how many races have you won on that streak of greased lightning, anyhow?"

"Six," Ponce answered quietly. "Just six."

The blue eyes widened. "*Just* six, the guy says! How many times have you started her?"

"Six."

The slender rider in crimson silks hitched himself around on the bench, regarding Ponce thoughtfully for a moment. "You take the cake," he stated finally. "Last winter you showed up out of nowhere and ran off with the Santa Anita Handicap on a filly no one had seen nor heard of before. You drop out of sight the next day. Then you show up here and proceed to win every stakes race you enter. And you act as if it was the most natural thing in the world!"

Ponce's eyes crinkled at the outer edges, and his lips parted in a slow smile. "You are the famous Bob Willis," he said. "How many races have you won?"

"Four hundred or so, I guess. Why?"

Ponce's smile widened. "My six against your four hundred are not very many, are they then?"

The seasoned jockey shook his head quickly. "Can't figure it that way, kid. I've been in the game for six years, and I've lost a lot more than I've won, I can tell you." He paused, his blue eyes twinkling. "With you, this winning business is getting to be a habit!"

Ponce glanced at the black circle of felt pinned to Willis' right shoulder. "Number 2," he said. "You ride the English horse, Trafalgar."

"I'm going to try to ride him," the other corrected him. "He's got a head that weighs a ton, and half the time he decides to try to walk the outside rail, just for the heck of it; but he's my baby today, bless him."

"Maybe," Ponce said slowly, "you and Trafalgar win this race, Bob Willis."

"Anything can happen in a race," Willis agreed without enthusiasm. "Maybe a big surprise will happen to me today; but just maybe."

"*Riders out!*"

At the sudden shout from the loudspeaker directly above his head, Ponce jumped a foot off the bench, then glanced quickly around to see if anyone had noticed his nervous reaction to the call. He rose and waited quietly until the first four riders filed past him. When Bob Willis touched him on the shoulder and said, "Good luck, kid," he nodded without speaking, because he could not trust his voice just then. Falling into line behind Number Four, he stamped his feet in their soft-soled boots to relax his legs and stepped along the short corridor.

A moment later, bright sunlight struck him as he walked down the narrow path leading to the saddling paddock. He blinked his eyes rapidly, then held them shut an instant. When he opened them, he saw the eyes of the crowd lining the path fixed on him. For a brief moment, then, anger touched him, anger at these people who stared so rudely at him, who seemed bent upon making him feel strange and out-of-place in this roaring White World into which Desert Storm had carried him.

In his expensive white and green silks, he looked like any other jockey in the line, except for the thick mass of wavy hair that fell in a black cloud well below his shoulders. It was the hair, he knew, that excited all the curiosity. Never before had a full-blooded Apache jockey participated in The Sport of Kings; or if he had, he had not worn his hair in the old-fashioned way, as Ponce did. "Don't let it worry you," he told himself for the second time that day. "Let them stare until their eyes cross, if it will make them happier."

The silent, police-guarded procession ended inside the saddling paddock. Each of the nine jockeys went to his mount for final instructions from owner and trainer. Ponce saw Desert Storm standing motionless in her wire mesh stall and stepped quickly to her. Moving alongside, he ran a hand over her hard rump, then jumped back as she shook her head angrily and lashed out at him with a rear foot. For a moment he just stood backed up against the board wall of the stall and stared at her, puzzled by her violent reaction to his touch. It was not the kicking action itself that held him still. He had yet to see a keyed-up Thoroughbred that did not frequently kick; Desert Storm was no exception. But her strike just now had not been the nervous stamping movement common to the mettlesome racer. It had been prompted by genuine anger and had been aimed at him.

As he studied her, realization of what troubled her came and he felt doubt creeping into him. All too clearly, the powerful black's mind was far removed from anything to do with today's race. No film of sweat glistened on her neck and shoulders to tell of her readiness and fitness. She was standing too straight and too calmly. And the bulging muscles on her shoulders and rump were rock-hard and still, instead of flaccid and quivering. All her attention was centered on a colt in the stall directly opposite her.

Gil Dreen's voice pulled Ponce out of the gloom into which his thoughts had plunged him. "Don't go too much by the way she's acting, son," the stocky trainer said quietly. "She'll move out when the time comes."

Ponce nodded absently, without replying. He knew, of course, that fillies regularly had "off" days, and Desert Storm had twice before been quieter in advance of a race than was good for his own peace of mind. She had not failed to come out of it when the gates crashed open, however. But she had never acted quite the way she was today. He stepped forward and again ran his hand along her side. He dodged back barely in time to escape the long yellow teeth as, with a savage snaking movement, she reached around and snapped at him.

He said sharply, "Quit that!" and slapped her with a flat-handed blow on the muzzle.

Again Gil Dreen spoke from his place at the filly's head. "She'll be all right, son. But I've got a suggestion to make, if you'd care to hear it."

Ponce moved closer to the famous trainer of the David Forrest Thoroughbreds. "Say the thing, please," he requested in a worried tone. "I don't like the way she acts this day."

"This is a mile and a half race, you know. She's not gone that distance before, and she's up against some pretty good routers,* like Trip-Up over there and this new English importation, Trafalgar. If I were you, I'd rate her pretty well back until you hit the half. Let her taste the bat a few times while you're holding her in; it will make her madder than hops. By the half, I think she'll be in a running frame of mind. If she'll move then, get to the leaders in the next quarter. Then, coming home, shake her up for all she's worth. She's going to need everything she's got."

Ponce had been nodding steadily while the other spoke. Twice he slapped his right boot with the thin whip of whalebone and looped leather. Now he glanced down and studied it as if he had never seen it before. Just once had he struck his filly with the bat. It had angered her out of all proportion to the sting itself; but it had served to make her mind her business more carefully. He said slowly, reluctantly, "I will use the bat this time; but only if she refuses to move out."

"Good enough," Gil Dreen said heartily. "Don't be too concerned, Ponce. Most of the other entries you've met before, and whipped. You'll do all right this time."

* A *Router* or *Route horse* is a distance runner, as opposed to a *Sprinter*, or a short distance runner.

Ponce did not appear to be listening. He was gazing through the meshing at a high-headed colt across from him. "That Number Eight," he said absently, "I have not seen him before."

"That's Trip-Up, the colt I mentioned a minute ago," explained Gil Dreen quickly. "They say he's fast and likes this mile and a half. It'll maybe pay you to watch him. I saw him working out a couple days ago, and I noticed he's got a lot of early foot."*

Ponce started to answer; but turned instead as a gigantic brown whirled directly behind Desert Storm and reared in an attempt to shake his two handlers loose. He was a rawboned colt, with mountainous shoulders and hindquarters, and it required the strenuous efforts of two men to control him as he flung himself about the narrow walking circle. Even as Ponce reached up and jerked Desert Storm farther into her stall, the brown reared a second time, holding his handlers a foot off the ground for an instant. Then he plunged down on all fours, shook his big blazed head savagely and allowed himself to be hauled on around the circle.

Ponce glanced at Gil Dreen and frowned slightly at the expression he read in the man's face. He questioned softly, "That is the Trafalgar you mentioned?" When Gil Dreen nodded silently, he said in the same soft voice, "You believe he will beat Desert Storm, I think."

The trainer did not speak for a long moment. He took a great breath, let it out slowly and looked squarely into Ponce's eyes. "I don't know, son," he said gently. "The best get beat sooner or later. You know that as well as I do. Let's just say you'd better keep an eye on him. And while you're about it, keep the other eye on his rider. Willis is one of the best in the game."

"I will do that," Ponce stated. He reached out and touched Desert Storm's neck firmly. When he spoke again, his words

* An expression denoting the fast getaway ability of a horse.

were for her alone. "I think maybe you and I will have to go pretty fast this time. Maybe faster than those other times."

"Reins over!" the loudspeaker commanded, and nine loops of leather flipped up and settled over nine necks.

"Riders up!"

Ponce raised his left foot, and when Gil Dreen put both hands under it, he grasped the tiny saddle and the reins and sprang astride. A moment later he was turning Desert Storm after Number Four in the procession heading out onto the track.

Throughout the parade up past the grandstand at a walk, Ponce centered all his attention on his filly, feeling her out with the sensitiveness of the true horseman. She moved altogether too quietly, as if she cared nothing at all about the coming race. Even when he lifted himself in the irons and put her to a slow canter up the track at the end of the parade, she showed no signs of eagerness. Halfway past the crowded stand, he flicked her slightly with the bat and barely missed being thrown head over heels as she downed her head and seemingly tried to stand on it while kicking holes in the air.

A spectator leaned over the steel fence holding the crowd off the track and shouted, "Ride 'em cowboy!" and another voice cried shrilly, "You're in the wrong show, Ponce! This is a race track, not an Arizona rodeo!"

Blushing furiously, Ponce pulled Desert Storm's head up and put her into a reaching canter that carried him away from the grandstand and the laughing crowd. Fifty yards onward, the golden chestnut Trip-Up went past, moving with a light grace that was sheer poetry.

In the backstretch, Ponce eased his mount to a walk and let his thoughts touch briefly upon the events of the last three months. In his mind's eye, he again saw the other tracks down which he had taken the filly to victory after victory, the other grandstands, and the other racers against which he had pitted the flying black from the desert. He admitted without vanity

that he and Desert Storm had become the most talked-of
figures in the sporting world since their initial appearance at
Santa Anita last February. With pardonable pride, he thought
of the talk going around the stables lately—the talk about
Desert Storm's having been nominated for the honor of Horse
of the Year.

His resolve to retire her after the almost-fatal race at Santa
Anita in which she had hemorrhaged had been short-lived. His
friend, Gabe Stuart, had found himself with a thousand head
of cattle on his hands and very little to graze them on this last
spring. The sparse rains had not brought the grass up as usual.
The whole desert country was burning up for lack of water.
Gabe's cattle would die by the hundreds, unless something
were done quickly.

And so Ponce had brought the overnight sensation out of
her brief retirement and had shipped her east for the rich
races of spring and summer. The purses she had steadily won
were paying for the machinery and labor going into the making
of irrigation canals and ditches. Those ditches came from the
mountains down into the foothills and desert, and brought
water for Gabe's land. Very soon now he, Ponce, and his filly
could go back there and commence work on the second half
of The Dream, which was the forming of a racing stable.
There would be money enough to purchase several good brood-
mares also, if today's race turned out like the others. If . . . if
Desert Storm would run . . .

Ponce pulled himself out of his daydream with a start as,
glancing ahead, he saw the other entries milling behind the
starting gate. With a frown for his carelessness, he shook
Desert Storm up and ran her down to take his place.

The starter was calling his name peevishly as he rushed up,
ordering him to take his filly in immediately. The narrow gate
snapped shut behind him. There were a few moments, then,
in which he could collect his scattered wits and set himself, as
the others were led into their proper gates. Even so, he had

barely enough time to note again that Desert Storm was unnaturally quiet and to worry about it before the deafening
jangle of the bell shattered the stillness, and the gates crashed
open.

"THEY'RE OFF!"

For the hundredth part of a second, nine gleaming bodies
lifted and hung suspended in the open gates. The line broke as
they came down and rushed for the turn in a scrambling wedge.
The roar of the crowd was beaten down by the thundering
hooves, the popping whips and the shrill cries of the riders, as
nine of the world's fastest Thoroughbreds struggled to take
the lead in the rich Arlington Special at Chicago. There was
one mile and one half to go. At the end of that gruelling distance, $100,000 waited to be claimed by the winner.

At the opening of the stretch, a long golden form flashed
out ahead of the close-pressed mass and started to open a lead
that grew unbelievably. The fast-breaking Trip-Up was running off with the race before it had gotten well under way.

Desert Storm had broken fast; but not as fast as some. Coming off the turn, she was running in sixth place. She moved
easily; but without force or fire, and Ponce realized before
she had taken a dozen strides that it would not be necessary
to restrain her at all. She was sided by two horses; but not
closely pressed or hindered in any way. When those two forged
ahead, Ponce signaled for more speed, but Desert Storm did
not respond. Another horse, moving out suddenly under whip
and heel, passed her. Ponce glanced back and tried to tell himself he was dreaming when he saw the track empty behind
him. Desert Storm was tailing the field!

He settled lower over the pounding withers. For another
eighth he waited for the well-known surge of power to be un-
leashed beneath him. Twice he shook the reins urgently, twice
he called sharply into the pointed ears, and twice he glanced
ahead and saw the field drawing farther and farther away.
With growing alarm, he drove his heels hard against the steel-

like ribs, and in the turn the sluggish filly made a half-hearted sprint that moved her up to the lagging horses in the rear of the field. There she settled; but only for an instant. As she straightened well down the backstretch, the whip slapped sharply against her rump, and she commenced to run with something of her old flashing speed.

Feeling her going, Ponce once again began to hope; but when he had her even with the front-running colts, she suddenly slowed her speed and paced them. She was on the outside, which meant that she would be forced to cover more ground in the turn, unless she could get out in front of the leaders and take the rail position.

A quick glance showed Ponce a frightening picture up ahead. The golden Trip-Up was streaking along like a beam of light through darkness under the pressure of his rider. He would be into the far turn in fleeting seconds. Ponce saw the cream-colored tail streaming out like a banner in the wind. From the way it remained straight, without any betraying circular lashing motion, it was apparent that Trip-Up still had plenty in reserve. Gil Dreen had been right when he had said the chestnut was fast and good for the mile and a half. He still maintained a six-length lead over the others.

Ponce threw the reins away* at the mile post. And for the first time he began to use the whip with methodical intent, knowing the blows would insult the sensitive filly beyond endurance, even though they produced no real pain. The looped leather popped on her rump like a gunshot, and she leveled out in a furious drive that left Ponce gasping for breath. But even as she moved out like a thunderbolt, a dark horse with a green hood over its blazed face moved with her.

For a moment Ponce was too concerned with getting Desert Storm in hand to notice anything else; but as he pulled her toward the inside rail, in preparation for the turn, he became

---

* An expression meaning to relax the grip on the reins so that the horse is running freely, without any restraint.

aware of that other horse. It was between him and the rail, and
it was running at Desert Storm's exact speed, making it impossible for her to cut in. Like perfectly timed machines the
pair took the turn. As always, Desert Storm lugged out badly,
falling a length off the pace. It was the one fault she had, and,
apparently, the one no amount of skillful riding and handling
could correct. When the track straightened, she was in the
exact center of it, a length and a half behind the driving brown.
It was then that Ponce saw the Number Two on the white
racing pad. It was then that he realized who had come up to
challenge Desert Storm.

Trafalgar!

Down the endless sweep of track the rawboned giant from
England was rocketing in a murderous drive to catch the still
strong-running Trip-Up. And with fear and uncertainty tearing
at him with icy hands, Ponce flung Desert Storm after him.
When the quarter pole flashed by he shook his head savagely.
The race was not finished yet!

"All right," he screamed into Desert Storm's flattened ears. "Get him! *Now!*"

He uncocked his whip again. It played a rapid tattoo about the sweating black shoulder, flank and rump, and Ponce reached up to snap his goggles down over his eyes as wind tears blinded him. Gauging the distance yet to be run, he dared not risk moving the filly in toward the rail. Trip-Up was less than two lengths in the lead now. He was running gamely under the whip; but foot by foot the ground was being cut out from under him by the two rear-runners who had come up to press him in the final sprint. Fifty yards beyond the quarter they caught him and took the lead.

And now it was Desert Storm and Trafalgar!

The filly had moved up to side the colt at the opening of the stretch, when Ponce had urged her; but she could not open up so much as an inch of daylight. Ponce glanced aside and saw Bob Willis measuring him and Desert Storm. Then the veteran jockey faced front and took to the whip with renewed vigor. Under that pressure, Trafalgar fled toward the finish line like an enraged stag seeking refuge from the hounds.

He went up, up. He was going on when Ponce seemingly went crazy. In the packed grandstand, the thousands of on-lookers fell silent at sight of a rider lifting his mount and hurling it toward the wire with hands, feet and bat.

Frightened half out of her wits by her rider's unusual be-havior, Desert Storm sought to run out from under him. She settled still lower, long legs blurring above the track, and all the power in her great body went into the battle to catch the English champion before he reached the wire. She could not do it. Over track and field a great moaning sigh went up as, watching the grim struggle below them, the spectators realized that the flying filly from the desert had met her match at long last.

A slight ridge in the track caused Trafalgar to waver to the right. It cost him precious inches. It cost him his lead. For even as he veered, Desert Storm summoned up the last vestige of strength in her and forged ahead to side him again. In an agony of determination, the two streaked for the wire, so close together their jockeys' feet touched.

The giant filly was running as if every stride would be her last; but she would not go down. She staved off Trafalgar's challenge and dueled with him down the last heartbreaking yards. Only once before had she been challenged as she was now being challenged. Only once before had defeat stared her in the face. Then she had struck out at it and brushed it aside. But now?

In a blinding sprint, she took the lead. She went up a quarter length, a half length. And she was going on with deadly intent as the pair flashed under the wire.

The crowd went wild. They were on their feet, screaming, whistling and stamping. They kept it up all the while Ponce and Desert Storm, shaken and drenched with sweat, faced the battery of cameras in the Winner's Circle.

Sitting the quivering, weaving filly, Ponce smiled obediently when the photographers asked him to. He pretended not to hear the questions flung at him from all sides, questions about his future plans for Desert Storm. It would do no good at all, he knew, to tell them the truth just now. Soon enough they would find out what he was going to do. And so he went on smiling and nodding, and he did not have to pretend to be happy.

Today Desert Storm had won over $100,000. It was enough.

2

Voice from the Grave

FOUR days after Desert Storm triumphed over Trafalgar in the Arlington Special, Gil Dreen's black Lincoln swept around a mesa and bore down on the narrow lane which cut away from the desert road. At the end of the lane, clearly seen in the distance, Gabe Stuart's white adobe ranch house sat atop its knoll.

From the moment they rounded the mesa, Ponce began to sit straighter and farther forward on the seat. His head turned constantly and his eyes widened in wonder at what he saw. Had it not been for the many well-known landmarks, he would have thought he was in an utterly unfamiliar part of the country. Where before the desert had reached, sear and brown, from the foothills in the north farther than the eye could see to the south, there was now a blanket of bright green. All over that cool blanket were glowing spots of color. Even the sage's lavender-gray tone had taken on a deeper, richer hue.

Ponce knew what water could do to the thirsty soil of the desert. A year ago, Gabe Stuart had sold the mesa section to David Forrest. In a month's time, water from the lake below the mesa had been released through ditches, and the section had been transformed into a green paradise.

Now Desert Storm's winnings had actually provided the

means whereby Gabe Stuart was enabled to hire irrigation units to come out from Tucson and dig a canal from Ocatillo River, down through his holdings. The result paralleled that of the Forrest irrigation system, but on a far bigger scale.

From the main canal, countless smaller ditches had been cut along the slopes of ridges lower down, and the water, spilling across the gently tilted land, had drawn greenness over the sandy soil. Desert flowers of numberless species roused to new life and lived on in surprise at this miracle. Some of them forgot their proper seasons and insisted on blooming continually.

Gil Dreen turned off the road, steered the Lincoln carefully along the narrow lane and slowed before the house. He chuckled at the sight of the lone figure rising slowly from the rawhide-bound rocker on the front porch. Ponce flung the car door open and leaped out, his face glowing with pleasure as Gabe Stuart continued to stand on the porch and stare unbelievingly at his visitors.

"We are home, Mr. Gabe!"

"Huh?"

The elderly rancher seemed unable to believe his eyes. For a long moment he stared, then gave voice to a yell that startled the chickens in their coop behind the house.

"Thunder an' lightenin'!" he roared, "Where in tarnation did you all come from all of a sudden?"

He grabbed up the saddle he had been working on, as if not knowing what else to do, dropped it and jumped off the porch to meet Ponce. His big arms went around the youth's shoulders and he dragged the boy about the yard in an awkward, bear-like dance, the while he continued to howl like a wounded desert wolf. They reeled into the side of the car and halted, panting for breath.

"Last I heard of you all and Desert Storm, you was jest about played out after snitchin' the purse from under old Trafalgar's nose in Chicago." He paused, his gaze going to the new van behind the Lincoln. Quickly he looked into Ponce's eyes again. "Nothin's wrong with the filly, is there, son? That race didn't hurt her, did it?"

Ponce shook his head, knowing that the rancher's concern was real. "Nothing is wrong with her," he said. "It is only that there is more than enough money now to pay for all this irrigation work you have had done, and enough to get some good brood mares. So we came home."

It was the truth, Gabe Stuart knew, so far as it went; but it did not go far enough. "I reckon I know another pretty good reason why you come back, son," he said quietly.

"But, I told you . . ." Ponce began.

"An' I heard the race on the radio," Gabe cut in. "The announcer said, good and clear, 'Ponce has taken the whip to Desert Storm.' " He paused, then finished gently, "You're not in the habit of doin' that."

Ponce glanced away. "The whip cannot hurt her," he said. "She was not trying very hard, so I struck her. It made her angry and she ran, then."

"Sure," Gabe murmured, "sure, I know. But I got a suspicion that you sort of figured it was time to give her a mite of rest, if it took a whip to make her mind her business."

"Even so," Ponce replied in vast relief at the other's understanding. "Even though the whip does not hurt her, I do not like to use it." He hesitated, debating whether to make a confession, and decided to speak honestly. "Even if it had hurt a little, I think I would have used it on her, Mr. Gabe. She was not really trying, and I knew all the time that she could outrun that Trafalgar. If I had not been so sure, I would not have pushed her."

Gabe Stuart closed one eye in a wink. "That's all I wanted to know, son," he said with a chuckle. "Now let's get her out of that fancy carriage. I'm hankerin' to have a good look at her."

Gil Dreen drove on to the stable, parked and came around to unlock the rear doors of the van. "I was just about to take this outfit, filly and all, on to Shady Mesa with me," he declared, extending a hand and grasping Gabe Stuart's leathery palm.

Gabe nudged Ponce. "Go on, son," he urged. "Bring her out. From all I've read and heard about her in the last three months, I reckon on seein' her grown to about forty hands and sportin' a pair of wings!"

Ponce stepped into the van and unchained the restless filly. "Here she comes!" he called. "Watch out behind!"

The words were followed immediately by violent action, as Desert Storm erupted through the narrow opening, struck the sand and whirled to bolt halfway across the yard. She skidded to a halt, pivoted and blew lustily through flaring nostrils. Then she bent her knees, dropped to the sand and rolled and flopped about, as if trying to bury herself in the warm earth.

Gabe regarded her with faint alarm. "Does she always go crazy like that?"

Both Gil and Ponce were laughing heartily as they watched the big racer squirm and grunt at her dirt bath. "Always," answered Gil. "Makes no fuss about getting in; but once those doors open, she comes out like she was running the Kentucky Derby in reverse."

Ponce said gravely, "I think she always remembers that other trailer from which there was no escape."

Both men nodded soberly. "Reckon that's it," Gabe agreed. He watched Desert Storm place her front feet firmly under her and lunge up, to stand and shake herself violently. When she moved toward them, he said, "She's thinner and harder than she was, I'd say. Looks like she was made of steel and elastic."

"Perfect condition," Gil stated proudly. "With very little work, she could be put on any track any time. She's one of those rare animals that thrives on hard work."

As if to show she knew she was the subject of conversation, Desert Storm arched her neck, lifted her head higher and posed before them for a moment. Then she reared and lunged past them, through the open gate of her paddock, there to spin about and race down its length.

Gil Dreen turned quickly and went to unhitch the trailer from his car. Climbing in behind the wheel, he said cheerfully, "I called my wife from Tucson and told her I'd be home for supper. If I don't get a move on, I'll hear about it for the next six months!" He pressed the starter and shifted gears, then spoke to Ponce. "Any time you want to take to the tracks again, son, just let me know. I can tell you right now that Mr. Forrest is expecting you to go to Santa Anita with us again this January, so don't let Desert Storm fall into one of these irrigation ditches!"

While the old rancher and the Apache boy smiled, he released the clutch and sped away across the yard. Moments later, a thick cloud of dust completely hid the Lincoln from view. When the cloud had disappeared in the distance, where Shady Mesa loomed like a gigantic purple shadow in the evening sky, Ponce and Gabe turned toward the house.

While they ate supper, and afterwards did the dishes, the rancher plied Ponce with countless questions about the races the boy had won on the world-famous Desert Storm. Ponce described each of them in detail, knowing that his old friend's interest in himself and the filly was equal to his own. For three hours they sat on the back porch and talked of all that had happened in the recent past. At last Gabe rose and stretched.

"It's way past my bedtime, son," he said between yawns. "Best we get some sleep and save some of this talk for another time, eh?"

Ponce jumped to his feet and started around the end of the house, toward his lean-to in the rear. At the corner he halted and turned to face the man who had become more than a friend to him. He said softly, "It is good to be home again, Mr. Gabe," and slipped from sight.

Some time between midnight and first dawn, Ponce found himself sitting bolt upright on the narrow cot in the lean-to. An instant before he had been sleeping soundly. Now he was wide awake, his every sense keyed to the night around him. One by one he singled out the sounds coming in through the open door—the dull thud of Desert Storm's hoofs in the sand as the filly paced up and down the length of her paddock in unfamiliar loneliness, the whisper of a bat's wings disturbing the cool air close to the house, the wild, lost cry of a coyote on some wind-swept ridge and the closer, louder call of an owl.

It was this last that had jerked him up from deep sleep, and he was off the bed and outside before he realized it. He stood in the faint light shed by the waning moon and stars and turned his head slowly back and forth, trying to pick up the sound again. The seconds ticked slowly past as he waited. And then it came once more, from somewhere over beyond the stable that sat between the house and barn. Before the call had ceased, Ponce was racing across the yard. He rounded the end of the stable, ran on across the stretch of moonlight and slid to a stop a dozen paces short of an old gray pony that stood all alone in the night.

Peering into the shadows rimming the walls of the stable and barn and the clumps of sage nearby, Ponce could see no

sign of any human being. And then the old gray pony switched
its tail and stamped, and a dry, gutteral voice said from the animal's black shadow, "Is it the way of the Apache to rush into
the night without weapons to fight one who might be an
enemy?"

The black shadow changed shape, and a strange figure
stepped into view at the pony's head. Moonlight made a silver
halo around the lowered head, and a stray breath of air whirled
across the knoll and lifted the tattered blanket so that the
ancient figure took on the aspect of some earth-bound bird
with ragged wings flapping.

Ponce was still breathing quickly from his run. He waited
until The Old Apache came away from the pony and stopped
within reach of him before replying, then said evenly, "When
the call came a second time, I knew The Great Joto had come.
That is why I carried no weapon, my father."

The withered hands came out from under the ragged blanket, and the old one took another step forward. He placed his right hand on the boy's head and intoned the Apache greeting.

"Do you walk in beauty, my son?"

"I walk in beauty, my father," Ponce answered quietly.

"Has there been pain and ugliness in your heart, my son?"

"There has been no pain nor ugliness in my heart, my father," Ponce murmured.

"*Enju*," the deep voice said. "It is well."

The age-old greeting ritual over, the two shook hands. Ponce looked into the sun-blackened face of this ancient man who had once been one of the greatest warriors of the Mimbreno Apache tribe and could see no sign of change. After so many years have written their stories upon a countenance, there is no room left for more writing. This was the way it was with Joto. No one of his people knew his real age. It was laughingly said of him that he was the first man in the world and that it was he who had told *Yosen*, the giver of life, exactly how to fashion the first Apache out of clay. When *Yosen* had done his bidding, the tale went, Joto was so well pleased with the result that he announced then and there, "He is so fine that I too will be an Apache," and so those two were the first Apaches in the world.

Thinking of the humorous myth, Ponce half smiled in the moonlight, and his eyes took on a mischievous twinkle. "How many seasons have you seen, my father?" he asked.

"Too many!" The Old Apache snapped. Immediately he knew that the youth was speaking in jest, and his own deep-set eyes sparkled. He cupped his hands, as though holding a little ball. "When the world was this big, I held it like this! Now you know what no one else has ever learned, the age of Joto." His wrinkled lips parted to disclose toothless gums in a grimace that passed for a smile with him, and his shoulders jiggled faintly with his silent laughter. "Sit down," he ordered abruptly.

Ponce sank to the sand, his legs crossed under him, and

The Old Apache squatted down facing him. For a moment neither spoke; then Joto announced matter-of-factly, "I have dreamed a dream."

Ponce bit back an exclamation of disappointment in the nick of time. Immediately he felt ashamed of his reaction, knowing Joto had not come here in the small hours of the night to recount some idle sleep-picture. Speaking carefully, in the formal dialect of the council, he asked, "Was it a good thing you saw, my father?"

The Old Apache moved his head slowly from side to side, and the network of deep wrinkles formed black lines on his forehead as he frowned "I know not," he muttered. "But this I know, my son; you and I will start out on a journey of two days' length when the sun rises above the world."

"A journey?" Ponce echoed. "Where?"

The other lifted a long, reed-like arm and pointed to the northwest. "There," he replied. "Along the mountains we will ride, then turn into them. Somewhere up there, we will stop. I know not where; but I know the way. And when we are come to the place, I will know it."

A chill ran down Ponce's spine, and he shivered. He well knew that The Old Apache did not do things out of a sense of sheer adventure. That there was some hidden purpose to the journey, he did not for an instant doubt. He asked slowly, "How came this dream to you, my father?"

In the fading light of the moon, The Old Apache's eyes peered out from their deep sockets, and his voice took on a low, wondering tone.

"Slowly, it came," he replied. "Four days ago there was silence all around me. The birds sang; but there was no sound. I threw a rock high into the air; but it made no noise when it struck the ground. The stream rushed past my wickiiup in silence, and though the trees bowed low before the wind, they whispered not at all." He paused, his eyes glittering blackly. "Believe you this?"

"I believe it, my father," Ponce whispered.

"*Enju!*" Joto grunted. For a moment, then, he paused to draw the picture sharply through his mind again. "For these four days I have eaten nothing. Yesterday, when the sun went down, I lay down before my dwelling and stared straight into the sky. How long I was there, I know not; but suddenly there was movement in the ground beneath me, and a voice came through the ground and into my ears. It said, 'Joto, my brother, take the young man who is become as your son and go toward the far hills. Ride without haste for two days. When the sun rests on the crest of the mountains, stop on the rim of the valley you will have found and wait for the gift to appear before you."

The deep voice sank into silence, and Ponce crouched in the grayness of first dawn and shivered. What wisdom lay hidden in the shrunken form of this once-mighty warrior, no one knew; but the legends about him were numerous and often told by the wise men of the Mimbrenos. For himself, Ponce could not doubt the hidden powers of Joto, because it was he who had healed Desert Storm's shattered foreleg when everyone else had said there was no hope of saving her. It was he who had foretold the filly's greatness, and that in itself was reason enough for Ponce's faith in him. After a long moment, he asked in a hushed voice, "Know you the voice that spoke to you, my father?"

The Old Apache nodded once. "I know; but I will not tell you yet. But know you this: of all Apaches, the one who spoke to me from the grave was the greatest, I think. I knew him well, and I say his lips knew not the way of untruth. We will do as he commanded me."

Ponce nodded. "So be it," he murmured.

The Old Apache rose to his feet and pulled the thin blanket closer about his bony shoulders. "We will wake Mr. Gabe and tell him. Come."

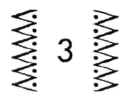

3

The Gift

THROUGHOUT the day they traveled steadily along the base of the Mogollons and at night made a dry camp in the brooding stillness of the mountains. At noon on the second day, The Old Apache left the desert and led the way into a maze of canyons, ravines and upturned slabs of sandstone. It was like passing from bright sunlight into the dimness of a windowless house. The blinding sun no longer glared up from the sand, but came sifting down through narrow, slit-like openings far overhead. The intense heat fell away gradually as the two horses climbed steadily upward.

On level ground, Desert Storm had refused to accommodate her long strides to the short, choppy ones of the bony gray; but as the going became increasingly steep and rough, she settled to a walk.

For the most part, the journey had been made in silence. The Old Apache seemed reluctant to talk, so Ponce held back the many questions seething inside him. He could not ignore one thing, however—his stomach. Unaccustomed to going long without regular intake, it had been rolling and growling since noon of the first day. Now it felt like an empty furnace, and at last he decided to speak frankly.

24

"I have great hunger, my father," he announced during a halt to breathe the horses. "When do we eat?"

The other's quick anger surprised the young Indian. "Have you gone so far from your people that you do not know their ways at all?" Joto demanded. "It is a rule that one shall take no food into his belly until a dream be finished." He saw the look of hurt and surprise that ran across Ponce's face, and his voice lost some of its harshness. "The dream will not be finished until the sun goes out of the sky, my son. You must hold your hunger from you until then."

"So be it," Ponce sighed, taking his belt up another notch. "I will try." After a moment of silence, he added doubtfully, "Even then, I do not see what we shall eat. We brought no food."

The Old Apache tapped the unstrung bow dangling from his shoulder and indicated the quiver of short arrows strapped to the sheepskin pad of his saddle. "There are these," he said, "and there are rabbits all over these mountains. Is it not good enough?"

"It *will* be good, maybe," the youth replied with a grin and nudged Desert Storm with his heel to move her out after the pony. He studied his surroundings with growing interest.

The Mogollon mountain range sprawled across the face of the country like a massive broken chunk of stone which the ancient gods of the Apaches had piled up to form breastworks during some world-shaking battle. Rugged and wild and fearsome, they rolled their hills and tossed their ramparts toward the intense blue sky. In the old days, they had been the favorite hunting grounds of certain tribes of the region, and still later they had provided a last refuge for the Desert People while the White Man-Apache war raged. From a distance, they looked barren and lifeless, and the casual tourist, passing swiftly through the land, gave them no more than a brief, uneasy glance. To Ponce's people they were old, well-known friends, holding long, cool valleys within their forbidding walls. The Desert People knew where to find the rushing streams of cool water, the deep, blue pools and the meadows fragrant with grass and wild flowers. And the lonely, wild cry of the wind sweeping across the towering crags was a never-ending song of the land itself.

Ponce roused from his thoughts as the ground tilted steeply. Glancing ahead, he saw The Old Apache become half hidden in deep shadow as the gray plunged into a canyon whose walls rose a hundred feet upward. At the top, these leaned inward until the sky was but a thin blue streak. The horses' hoofs struck echoes from the floor, echoes that bounced back and forth and clattered on in magnified bursts of sound, far ahead. After an hour of steady climbing, the canyon widened, and the walls sank until they were mere banks. The Old Apache reined abruptly to the left and put his pony to a steep climb onto a long, flat bench.

Ponce followed, holding Desert Storm to a quick, scrambling walk with difficulty. He gained the bench and looked up at the sheer cliff overhanging the narrow ledge, then sent his gaze to the left and gulped when he found himself looking into a seemingly bottomless chasm. He could see no way off this bench, and he called out, "There is no trail, my father! See how the cliff blocks the other end?"

His traveling companion gave no sign that he had heard; but jogged steadily along the dangerous stretch of time-polished stone. He was a hundred feet distant as Ponce took another uneasy look into the dark depths of the chasm. When next he looked up, Joto had disappeared.

The youth pulled the filly to a halt. For a brief moment he sat in the shadow of the cliff and peered through the gloom, perplexed by the other's disappearance. Desert Storm was of a more practical bent; also, she owned the inherited trait of all horses, which was a violent dislike for being separated from her own kind. Without hesitation, she trotted along the bench, turned sharply where the wall showed a narrow slit and entered a cave-like passage. The walls here were so close that Ponce's knees brushed against them, and when he threw back his head and looked up, he could not see the sky. A hundred feet onward, the light died completely, and Ponce shortened his grip on the reins and rode warily, letting the filly make her own way along the upward-sloping passage.

For a quarter mile the darkness held, then a tiny circle of light glimmered far ahead. Coming at last into the open, Ponce was tempted to shout in sheer relief; but he pressed his lips together and cantered after The Old Apache, who was now far ahead and urging his pony up a narrow trail that cut along the perpendicular face of a yellow cliff. Arriving at the foot of that cliff, Desert Storm hesitated, tossing her head; but at a touch of Ponce's heels, she crouched and took to the dangerous climb like a big cat. Pebbles and dirt, loosened by her hoofs, flew out and showered down in thick bursts, striking up faint echoes on the floor far below.

For three more hours they climbed into the Mogollans, working their way into rougher, wilder country, where birds wheeled high overhead and where roaring streams crashed and rolled thunder between the broken walls and cliffs. The air grew thinner and colder, and the progress slowed as the strain took its toll on the horses' strength. Surprisingly, The Old Apache's pony proved far more adept at this kind of travel than did Desert Storm. The bony animal appeared to be made of steel and rawhide, and the breathing spells it required were far fewer than those demanded by the powerful black. Yard by yard, she was left behind, until Ponce could no longer see Joto nor hear him.

Gaining the top of a cliff by means of a terrifyingly narrow and steep trail, Ponce drew up to let Desert Storm catch her wind. They were at the lower end of a narrow strip of sand. On both sides, at the mile-distant end, towering walls enclosed the lifeless spot. A dull roar beat at the young man's ears. At first, he thought the altitude was responsible; but, looking toward the far wall, he spied a thick jet of water curving down-ward from its summit, and, though he could not see the pool at the base, he knew that the roar came from there.

Ten minutes later, he drew up at the edge of the foaming pool into which the waterfall plunged with a noise like thunder. A fine spray settled over him and his mount, cooling and refreshing them after the heat of the climb.

A careful survey of the surrounding walls disclosed no way out; but since The Old Apache had obviously passed along here and was now absent, Ponce reasoned that he had not flown out and must, therefore, have ridden on. He studied the damp ground for hoofprints. A moment later, he guided Desert Storm along the pony's trail. He was intently watching the ground, and so had no warning of the narrow gorge until darkness engulfed him. He halted, looked back at the sunlit canyon, then peered before him into the darkness. Another tunnel-like opening led into the side of the wall. After a few moments' hesitation, he urged Desert Storm ahead and felt her withers lift sharply under him as the floor tilted steeply again.

The passageway seemed endless. Twice Ponce found it necessary to halt the filly, when her breathing became labored. During the second pause, he glanced at the luminous dial of his wristwatch and saw that the hands indicated the hour of six. Alarmed, he stared at them, knowing that sunset was less than an hour away. The possibility of reaching a valley of any kind before this time seemed remote indeed. Could it be that The Old Apache had erred this one time?

He pushed the thought away and put Desert Storm into motion once again. She scrambled upward, grunting and snorting with the effort. When it seemed to the anxious boy that the passageway would never end, a speck of blue sky glimmered far ahead. This time he did shout with relief, and the noise of his voice crashed down about his ears like thunder. Terrified, Desert Storm threw herself into a scrambling, jumping run that took them out of the tunnel in a clattering rush.

The coolness of this high region was like a morning breeze. Both boy and horse breathed quickly and deeply of the pine-scented air, then the breath stopped in Ponce's throat as he took in the magnificent scene before him.

Miraculously, the broken country had fallen away behind them. There was a long mountain plain to the north. Encircling mountains were distant, low purple lines, and the plain itself lay like an accidentally-placed desert on all sides. A mile away, a thin finger of stone rose a hundred feet above the grassy floor; yet, upon closer inspection, it proved to be no single mass of rock at all, but a narrow mesa. Less than a mile in width, it stretched along the floor of this mountain desert, extending until the shadow along its eastern side sank to the thinnest of pencil lines in the blue haze of late afternoon.

Sitting there staring, Ponce saw a small, light-colored object moving up along the face of stone at a sharp angle. He jumped Desert Storm into a sudden run, excitement racing through him. With that excitement, there was a feeling of shame also, because he had doubted that the promised valley would appear before the sinking of the sun this day. He reached the foot of the mesa and looked up to see The Old Apache disappearing over the rim. Desert Storm took the perilous incline like a mountain goat. Minutes later, they reached the rim, and the boy saw Joto sitting his sweat-drenched pony less than ten feet away.

"You go too swiftly, my . . ." Ponce began, but he left the sentence uncompleted as he came alongside the other and glanced down.

The narrow ledge on which they sat was actually the top of a stone wall enclosing a valley some ten miles long and less than a mile wide. Directly below, the wall dropped two hundred feet to the level, grassy floor. Rimming the narrow valley, like sentinels at attention, were thick mountain pines. Their dark green branches contrasted sharply with the lighter green of the tall grass which covered the earth like a soft blanket.

Far to the north, the waning sunlight glinted on water. It was impossible to determine the exact size of the lake; but it appeared to lie almost in the middle of the valley. Extending from wall to wall, it acted as a line which cut the steep-walled retreat into two parts.

For long minutes Ponce sat there, taking in the scene, finding it almost impossible to accept, even with all of it so clear before him. He remembered the doubt that had come to him earlier in the day.

"You were right, my father," he said quietly. "Only I . . ."

"Doubted."

The Old Apache turned knowing eyes on him. A half smile changed his withered face, and he extended a clawlike hand to lay it on Ponce's shoulder. "Let it not trouble you, my son," he said. "With age comes faith, and you are still very young. One day you will learn to believe in those things your eyes cannot see."

He turned his gaze westward, and the smile died from his face. He looked all around, as if searching for something he had known would be here. Again he looked westward, a frown pulling his whitened brows low over his deep-set eyes. A narrow patch of crimson lay between the bottom edge of the sun and the highest peak of the Mogollans. He said in a vaguely irritated voice, "The time draws near."

Ponce looked at the thinning strip of sky. Just as the sun touched that distant peak, he glanced at Joto and caught his breath quickly, a chill rushing over him.

The Old Apache sat stiffly in his ragged saddle, his face lifted to the darkening sky. Suddenly he raised his arms and spread them wide, so that the blanket slipped off his shoulders. He said in a louder voice, "The time draws near!" A moment later, he cried out sharply, as if in pain, "My brother! The time is now! Why do you not come to me?"

Never before had Ponce seen The Great Joto show such emotion. He could not tear his eyes away from the contorted features. The usually blank-faced warrior was suffering from some inner torment that changed his whole being and made him for an instant like a lost child. Without understanding what was happening, Ponce knew that it had to do with Joto's voice from the grave. He thought blindly, *it must happen quickly, or his faith will be destroyed!*

The Old Apache's voice cut the air like a striking hand.

"Quickly! Get you into those trees!"

Ponce whirled Desert Storm toward a clump of pines fifty feet away, on a broad expanse of the ledge, The Old Apache following. They dodged around a ragged boulder and were in the trees. Then Desert Storm was rearing in fright as Joto leaped to the ground and grabbed her bridle.

"Hold her!" he commanded in a whisper. "Hold her! There must be no sound!"

The boy slid to the ground, took a short grip on the reins and drew the frightened filly close. Then he saw Joto crouching behind the big rock, one hand clamped over the pony's muzzle. He followed the other's example, drawing Desert Storm in behind the rock and craning his neck around an outcropping to see what had caused this wild flurry. It was less than a minute before the sound of someone climbing the trail to the ledge reached his ears.

He had seen no path leading into the valley; but the sounds were coming from the inside wall. They came closer, grew louder, and then Ponce bit his lips until he tasted blood as a gray stallion came into view before him.

One moment there was nothing visible but the expanse of purple evening sky. Then, the stallion was standing like a gigantic statue between Ponce and that sky.

There was something terrifying in the way he stood there, with the dying sun drenching his great body in bloody light. He faced south, his finely chiseled head upflung on its massive neck. Wind, streaming from the north, caught the heavy silver mane and tail and swept them in a wildly tossing cascade

along the heaving side and over the dark eyes. Ponce took the
stallion's measurements with knowing glance and realized that
he stood well over seventeen hands high.

At first he looked black; but in the red light that poured
over the mountain plain, it was difficult to determine his exact
coloring. Then, the big body moved and stood quartering
toward the stone that hid the two Indians, and Ponce saw
that the stallion was a dark gray, with black stockings that
gradually faded and changed into countless perfect dapples
along the bulging shoulders and hind quarters.

Every line and curve of the towering form bespoke breeding
of the highest order. No wild mustang grew to such size and
flawless conformation. No impure blood could produce legs
like slender bands of steel such as the gray possessed. Without
scar or blemish, he poised there, outlined against the sky, like
some forbidding giant from another world. And his wildness
hovered over him and filled the air about him like a heavy,
frightening scent.

For a full minute he remained in the fading light, then
moved, turning on the ledge to face into the wind. He swung
his head slowly from side to side, vaguely disturbed by something he sensed but could not identify. The wind was against
him, carrying no hint of danger; still, he keened the air, trying
to sift some message from it. During one circling movement of
his head, he faced the grove of pines and the large rock, and
for a paralyzing moment Ponce stared into the dark, glittering
eyes. It seemed impossible that those eyes could fail to pene-
trate the shadows, and the boy waited in an agony of suspense for some deadly movement of that proud being. But
after a moment, the head swung back, pointing upwind again.

Ponce was trembling from head to feet. Perspiration poured
from his body. He closed his eyes and clamped his jaws hard
in an effort to steady his nerves. When he looked up again,
the stallion was gone.

He rose and was starting around the rock when The Old Apache's hand gripped his arm and stopped him.

"Wait! He must not hear you nor see you!"

Ponce settled back. The minutes crawled by. The sounds made by the descending stallion faded gradually, then ceased altogether. When the silence was complete, Ponce left the protection of the boulder and led Desert Storm to the spot the stallion had occupied. Looking down, he saw the narrow trail that led to the valley. Sweeping the grassy plain below, he could see no sign of any living creature. Then, a band of eight horses trotted out of the pines fringing the left wall and started up the valley. An instant later, a gray form flitted into view, and Ponce recognized the gigantic stallion. Like a shadow, it rushed along the rear of the little band, moving effortlessly after them as they broke into headlong flight.

The reins were torn from Ponce's hand by Desert Storm's sudden lunge. He whirled and, with The Old Apache's aid, succeeded in recapturing her and dragging her back from the narrow trail.

"She would follow the gray one," Joto said, chuckling drily.

He stroked the filly's wet neck. Suddenly he ceased, turned to the north and became utterly motionless. After several minutes, he lifted his arms as before and began to speak in a strange, sing-song tone.

"My brother, whose name must not be spoken as your name, I heard your voice and obeyed, and I thank you for the gift which you have placed in the hands of this youth who is as my own son. In your gift your spirit lives, and so it shall be that your name shall live again. On that day when you and I stood where now I stand, you said that you would return. For the truth that was ever in you, I give you thanks, even as I give you thanks for your gift, the stallion which shall bear the name *Victorio*."

The last word was uttered in a wildly piercing tone. It seemed to hang in the air above the valley, like an invisible bird with strongly beating wings. Then it ran down the breeze and was lost in the deepening night.

"Victorio." Ponce repeated the name in a hushed voice, rolling the syllables on his tongue, as if savoring them. "It means *The Victorious One*, does it not?"

"Even so."

"And it is the name of he whose voice came to you in the night, is it not?"

"Even so," Joto murmured again. "The greatest warrior of the Apache nation. He was never defeated." His voice took on a deeper, stronger timbre. "I rode with him to war many times. He was the greatest, my son."

"I have heard stories of his victories, and the terrible one of his death. Because of him, the name *Apache* lives on." Ponce hesitated, then went on more slowly. "I do not understand one thing, my father."

"Say that thing."

"You said to the spirit of that warrior that the stallion is in my hands."

Joto nodded slowly, his white hair faintly shining in the gloom. "Even so. Time is a little thing that one may hold in one's hand, know you. I see what I see."

"But I do not."

"There is a saying among our people," Joto stated "When a man looks only with his eyes, all trails lead into the middle of nowhere." He stopped, watching Ponce closely, then said more sternly, "Think on that, my son."

"And so I will, my father."

On the point of going to his pony, Joto hesitated, then turned and spoke more gently. "We have another saying. 'To bring a wall to the ground, one has but to find one certain stone.' Think on that, too, my son."

The Mustañeros

AT THE foot of the trail outside the stone-walled valley they sat in the light of the small fire and devoured the remains of the big jackrabbit which Joto had snared. It had been roasted over the coals without salt or any other seasoning. Still, Ponce thought that he had never tasted anything half so good.

Beyond the firelight, Desert Storm and the old pony moved through the sage, taking short, broken steps because of their hobbles as they grazed on the sun-cured grass. With good forage for the animals and with the small pool of icy water that bubbled up at the foot of the cliff, this provided an ideal camping site. The scent of pine and juniper and sage was heavy in the night wind which boomed down across the mountain plain. Now that he had eaten his fill, Ponce could have lain back and fallen asleep . . . almost. All too many questions clamored for utterance, however, for him to relax now.

For the past hour he had been questioning The Old Apache about ways and means of capturing wild horses; but the answers had been extremely brief. Sometimes they had been mere grunts. Sometimes they did not come at all.

Joto sat hunched over, staring into the flickering fire, his

brows drawn to a sharp point above his nose. He had been
that way for a long time, and Ponce dared not break in upon
his thoughts. When Joto was thinking, it was best to let him
go on thinking.

"It is impossible to construct a trap such as many wild
horse hunters use," he stated suddenly. "In the first place, that
Victorio would watch everything that went on, and he would
probably tear the trap down as fast as it was built. In the
second place, he would never be fool enough to walk into a
trap, however carefully the entrance was concealed." He shook
his head. "No, a trap is not to be thought of."

Ponce remembered the lake lying in the center of the
valley. "If we could force him into the water, we could make
him swim until he was too tired to run, maybe."

The Old Apache's reply to that was a loud snort of con-
tempt. "I would hate to see you try to get close to that gray
devil in the water," he said. "He would kill you before you
could lift a hand."

Ponce rose, completely silenced, and went into the darkness
for more sage twigs to add to the fire. When he returned,
Joto was sitting up straight and staring intently at the blank
mesa wall before him. "Have you ever heard of a people known
as *Los Mustañeros?*" he asked, and when Ponce shook his
head, he motioned him to the ground.

"Long ago, before you were born," he began in the peculiarly
musical cadence of the experienced story-teller, "there were
great herds of wild horses all over the land. They were called
mustangs. For many years they had run free and grown in
numbers. It was seen by the White Man who came into the
land that they were swiftly becoming too numerous, and so
they were killed by the hundreds. So many were killed, in fact,
that it was not long before only a few herds remained. These
fled far to the south, into the region now known as Southern
Arizona, New Mexico and Texas. These remaining mustangs
had become wise in the ways of avoiding man. They were the

strongest and the swiftest of all. That was why they were still alive and free. It was very hard to catch them."

He paused, having set the stage for the picture he would now draw before his listener's eyes. Ponce had never heard him speak so before. He was completely fascinated by the ancient warrior's gift of words. His eyes were fixed on the dark features that seemed chiseled from stone in the firelight. Knowing full well that Joto had some deep and clear purpose in telling him this story, he waited.

"Now, the *mustañeros* were people from Mexico who went about the land in small groups which often consisted of but one family of five or eight souls. They were not very good fighters, these *mustañeros*; but they had a way with horses like no one I have ever known. They lived in ragged tents or brush wickiiups, and they made their living by catching the wild mustangs and selling them to the great rancheros in Mexico. Always they had one very swift horse that was trained to do a very special thing. And always there was one member of the family who was trained for this same special thing. He must be very slight, a very good rider and very brave. Sometimes the special *mustañero* was a girl-child. Indeed, some of the finest were girl-children.

"These families would find a herd of wild horses and follow them until they learned all the habits and feeding places of the band, then they would proceed to trap them. Usually, the leader and a few of the wisest and swiftest mares would escape capture, and it was then the *mustañeros* performed the deed which gave them their name.

"The fine, strong racer was led out and the young boy or girl who was to do the fearful deed was placed upon the racer and sent to where the leader of the wild band was known to be. All the family rode out to watch."

Again The Old Apache paused, taking a moment to picture the whole thing clearly in his mind's eye. He said then, "One such race I remember well. I saw many; but I remember this one best, because the rider was a girl-child of only twelve summers. She came from a family in which only the women had been *mustañeras*, and her mother, growing too heavy to ride the racers, had taught her the art. I will tell you how it went that day."

"The young girl-child waited inside the brush dwelling until her father called to her. When she came out, she carried in her hand a length of rawhide reata. Her father picked her up and placed her astride a tall roan mare that wore neither bridle nor saddle. With her knees, the girl-child turned the mare and guided her up a long, flat plain lying between steep walls of stone. No one told her what to do, and no one went with her. She was but twelve summers in the world, mind you, and a girl-child.

"We all rode to the edge of the plain to watch. After a long time, we saw a dust cloud sweeping down the valley, and then we saw five horses running before that cloud. Of the girl-child and the roan mare there was no sign. The five wild ones came on until they were halfway down the valley. They were fast, and they ran all in a straight line, as though racing for some fine prize.

"Suddenly, the roan mare appeared from beneath the cloud of dust, running like no horse I had ever seen before.

"She came steadily up to the five wild ones, and when they did not make room for her in their line, she bit one of them on the rump. It was clear to us, then, that the leader, a great sorrel stallion, had not been running his swiftest, for when the mare's teeth raked his rump, he darted out in front of the others, like a hunting arrow speeding from the bow. He left them quickly behind; but he did not leave the roan mare. He sank so low to the ground that his belly seemed to touch it, and his long legs moved so swiftly that we could not see them. Still, he could not outrun the mare. But she could not catch him either . . . we thought.

"I did not see the girl-child until the mare bit the stallion.

She was curled up like a ball, high on the big mare's shoulders, and she was almost hidden in the mare's long mane. When it seemed the mare could not outrun the stallion, I saw the girl-child move one hand very gently up along the straining neck. It was a signal. The mare seemed suddenly to fly over the ground, and before the heart could beat swiftly ten times, she and the stallion were running side by side. It was at this moment I heard myself shouting like an excited boy.

"When the mare had matched her stride perfectly to that of the mighty stallion, the girl-child doubled a leg under her, leaned out to grasp a handful of the sorrel's mane and pushed herself over onto the stallion's back.

"For a while the two horses raced on, as if tied together; then the mare veered away and ran back toward the camp, while the stallion flew on with the girl-child clinging to his back. He was but a tiny speck far down the plain, and I feared for the girl-child's life. And then I saw the sorrel commence to turn in a wide circle at the valley's far end. He was still running; but not so swiftly. After a long, long time, he came back up the valley, trotting slowly, his head almost touching the ground. He came closer, and I could see that the girl-child had thrown the reata over his nose and had fashioned a hackamore with which she guided him. She had done this the moment she had slipped from the mare to his back, and she made him go on running long after his wildness was dead in him."

The story ended, and Ponce discovered that he was gripping his hands together so tightly that his whole body was shaking. He was breathing swiftly, living each instant of the great race, as if it were happening before his very eyes. He even forgot to resent the central figure's having been a girl. He felt a great longing for the days of the distant past when such fearful deeds were regarded matter-of-factly by those who witnessed them.

"The sorrel stallion," he urged, "what became of him?"

The Old Apache smiled, remembering. "Three moons later

I saw him," he answered. "He was chasing a white stallion, and the same girl-child was riding him, as she had ridden the roan mare."

"Did he catch him?" Ponce asked, his eyes glowing in the dying firelight.

The ancient head moved slowly from side to side. The stern features darkened.

"No. He was almost up to the white one's shoulder when he suddenly stumbled. It was very rough country they were running in—covered with rocks of every shape and size. Had he slowed ever so little, even, he might have regained his footing; but he was determined to catch the white stallion. The girl-child was at that moment bending her leg under her for the change to the white. When the sorrel fell, she could not throw herself free. I stood and watched that great red horse rise high in the air and turn end over end, like a broken wheel. *And I saw him crash onto his back among the jagged rocks and crush the life from that brave girl-child, that silent, wonderful mustañera.*"

The last words were spoken in a hoarse whisper. After they had died, the tiny bed of coals sank lower and lower, and the night wind moaned above the lonely plain like the voice of a lost giant weeping. Tears stung Ponce's eyes, rolled down his cheeks; but he was not ashamed. In the dimness, he could see The Old Apache's sunken eyes. There were tears in them, also.

The silence ran on and on while the two of them sat staring into the past.

"Could *you* be a *mustañero*, my son?"

The question was like a rude hand slapping Ponce across the face. He started violently, his head coming up and back, his hands going suddenly cold.

"You mean for the gray stallion?" he asked.

"Even so."

Things were moving too swiftly. Ponce tried to reach out and halt the wild circling of his thoughts; but they escaped

him, leaving him silent and cold. He felt, rather than saw, The Old Apache's eyes on him. They were like icy fingers, pushing him toward a decision.

"Well?"

Ponce tried to move his head in denial; but he was as if paralyzed. He tried to frame a "no" with his lips; but his facial muscles were dead. In the utter stillness, his thoughts went back to this day's sunset. Again the massive gray stallion loomed threateningly against the purple sky. Again he heard Joto chanting his thanks to that vanished warrior who had led them to this place. And yet again the stallion stood before him, fixing him with those dark, wicked eyes that bored deep into him, as if probing for the suspected shadow of fear. Staring into the set eyes, he felt himself weakening, felt himself slipping toward the edge of the precipice.

"No," he whispered, "no, I am not afraid."

Only then did the stallion's piercing eyes lose their threatening glare. They softened, faded and were blotted out.

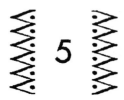

5

The Hunters

A COUNCIL of war was in progress in the cool richness of David Forrest's mansion at Shady Mesa. The tall owner of one of America's richest racing stables paced back and forth before the big fireplace, his handsome face thoughtful and faintly worried. He was the supreme commander, and his generals sat silently before him, waiting for his decision.

Gil Dreen, the wise and trustworthy trainer of the Forrest Thoroughbreds, would not voice an opinion until his employer gave him a hint of his own. Joe Marino, the slight Italian jockey who had abandoned the life of professional rider to work as assistant trainer and rider of none but Forrest racers, kept his dark eyes on the rug at his feet. Like Gil Dreen, he would not be the first to speak; but unlike the older man, he was finding it difficult to hold his tongue. Gabe Stuart, the kindly sheep-man-turned-cattle-rancher, who was like a father to Ponce, held his silence out of politeness. There was no doubt in his mind as to what he would do. Barbara Forrest, the slender, tom-boyish girl of sixteen, was not in the habit of interrupting her father's train of thought, so she bided her time, her little chin stubbornly set.

The sixth member of the council was a very tired-looking Apache named Ponce. He was silent, because silence was a

habit with him and because he had already spoken at great
length. Now he watched the owner of Shady Mesa pacing
back and forth and waited for words he feared to hear, words
that would bring his carefully wrought plans crashing down
about his ears.

David Forrest had been at his pacing for a quarter hour,
and he was beginning to get a little tired. A year ago, he would
have laughed outright upon hearing the story Ponce had related this morning; but a year had taught him to think twice
before laughing at anything the handsome young man said.
It was fantastic, the gift Ponce had for putting his finger on
a thing that baffled everyone else; fantastic how very much he
could say with so few words. Still . . . this story of his was the
most fantastic of all. David Forrest caught himself shaking
his head. No, the *most* fantastic part of it all was Ponce's
quietly-voiced request. He struck a fist into an open palm and
turned abruptly to face his silent watchers.

"You say it will be necessary to run this gray giant down?"
he asked for the tenth time. "And with three horses?"

Ponce's head moved ever so little. "Even so, Mr. Forrest."

"You think it can be done?"

Again Ponce's head moved. "The Great Joto says it can be
done," he answered quietly, "and so it can be done."

That stopped the tall man for a moment. "Oh," he
mumbled, started to pace again, thought better of it and went
back to his questioning.

"You want Joe, here, to ride The Iron Duke. May I ask
which of my other horses you'd like?"

"Last Laugh," Ponce replied quietly and kept his eyes carefully level with the corner of the fireplace as a look of amaze-
ment appeared on David Forrest's face.

"*Last Laugh!*" The man choked on the name. "You saw me
write out a check for $40,000 for that filly less than six months
ago, and you say, 'Last Laugh' as you would say, 'Pass the
gravy, please'!"

He choked again, took out his handkerchief and blew noisily into it. Ponce waited until he was certain his voice would not betray him, then said calmly, "Next to The Iron Duke, she is the fastest, is she not?"

"She is that!" Gil Dreen broke in suddenly, unable to resist rushing to the defense of his newest threat to the racing world. "And it might be she won't be *next* to The Duke, if she keeps improving like she has been lately. She'll give your black a run for her money one day, my lad."

At this friendly challenge to Desert Storm's supremacy, Ponce momentarily forgot the business at hand. He smiled at the belligerent trainer. "The day you name for the race to prove that," he said quietly, "Desert Storm will be there."

"Here! Here!" David Forrest cut in, laughing. "Let's not get sidetracked on *that* again! We'll all see which filly is the better one when the time comes." He swung back to face Ponce. "You say each of the three horses would have to chase this wild stud three miles or so over rough, rocky ground?"

"No," Ponce answered, wondering how many times he had already described the valley and the planned race. "The Iron Duke would run him less than three. Last Laugh would have less than two. The lake which Victorio will have to swim is a quarter mile wide. I will be waiting with Desert Storm at the lower end of it." He paused, then said with deliberate emphasis, "And the ground is *not* rough or rocky. It is perfectly level, with thick grass to cushion the hoofs. It is better than any track I have seen."

This last was of utmost importance, as everyone well knew. No horseman, worthy of the name, would risk damaging the delicate bones and tendons of his racers' legs—the Thoroughbred's weakest point—by running them over unsafe terrain. David Forrest knew Ponce well enough to be certain the Apache would not lie about such an important thing. He nodded, making a humming noise in his throat. His gaze swung to his trainer.

"Well, Gil? What do you think?"

"They're your horses, Mr. Forrest," Gil Dreen replied.

"They're more yours than mine," David Forrest stated laughingly. "You train them. I just own them."

The stocky, ex-rider drew a long, slow breath, looked all around and took the plunge. "All right, then. If Ponce says the footing is good, that's enough for me. I'll go along, if The Duke and Last Laugh go. It sounds like a crazy, wonderful thing, and I'd like to see it."

There was a sudden stirring of the tense figures seated before the fireplace; but David Forrest lifted a hand for silence and turned to the grinning Italian jockey. "How do you feel about this, Joe? You want to play mus— What's the word, Ponce?"

"*Mustañero.*"

"*Moos-tan-yero,*" David Forrest repeated, grinning at his own pronunciation of the word. "What's your verdict?"

The jockey was rubbing his hands together, like a batter approaching the plate. He caught the young Apache's eye and winked. "If Ponce wants me to start the ball rolling, I'll see if The Duke can get within shooting distance of that gray stud." He paused, winking again, this time at David Forrest. "But what am I supposed to do when The Duke runs this stud down within a mile, which he's apt to do? I haven't kept up on my trick riding lately, and I don't figure to jump into the middle of Ponce's Victorio, if I can help it. Maybe I'd better let the stud chase *me!*"

Ponce said with a grin, "If The Iron Duke can catch him, he can run away from him; so you will not have to worry, Joe."

"All right," said David Forrest, "that makes three votes for Victorio's downfall; but it gives us only two riders. Gil, which of your exercise boys would be likely to go for the idea?"

Barbara came off the divan, as if a pin had stuck her. "Exercise boy, my foot!" she cried indignantly. "I work as many horses as any old boy on this place, and I'm not going to sit in the grandstands this time!" She paused, out of breath, then grasped her father's arms. "Please, Dad! I've ridden Last Laugh practically every day since you bought her. I know her like a book, and she'll run for me. I don't weigh as much as the boys, either. Let me ride her. Please!"

For a moment the horseman looked down into his daughter's pleading eyes, then he spoke over the top of her brown head. "How about it, Ponce? Does she go?"

Ponce shook his head violently, the story of the Mexican girl coming sharply to him. What if the tall chestnut filly fell with Barbara? He closed his eyes at the thought, knowing he would never forgive himself if anything happened to this beautiful, laughing girl. But at that instant Barbara turned her wide brown eyes on him, and he stopped shaking his head. He said softly. "The greatest of the *mustañeros* was a girl-child. Let Barbara go with us."

Barbara shouted, jumped over and threw her arms around him. "Oh thank you, Ponce!" she exclaimed. "I'll do just as you tell me. You'll see!"

Ponce's face grew scarlet, and his eyes widened until they seemed about to pop from his head. He started to spring to his feet, but Barbara's arms held him fast, and he fell back, blushing harder than ever.

"Hey!"

Everyone whirled to stare at Gabe Stuart, who was glaring around indignantly. "Just where do I fit into this here picture?" he demanded. "I'm not about to stay behind and wait for news to sift in on the evenin' breeze. What do I do?"

Ponce was obliged to wait for the laughter to die down before replying. "You fit in at the end, Mr. Gabe," he said. "Victorio must be roped, once I have ridden him to the end of the valley. The Great Joto said he would call in some of the young men who are hunting in the mountains. With them, you must do the most important work of all, capture Victorio without injuring him, then get him into the corral."

"There's a corral?" Gabe asked.

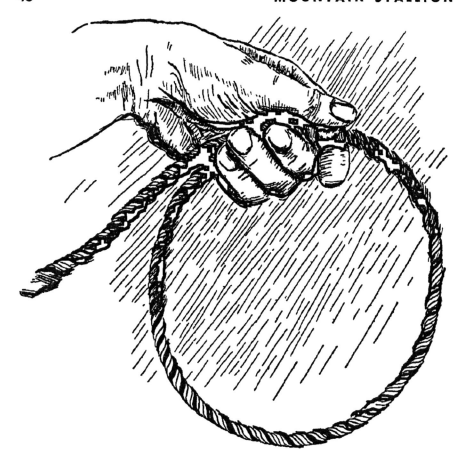

"There will be. Everything will be made ready before the chase."

David Forrest again called for attention. "It seems my vote no longer counts," he said, and chuckled. "All right. We go. Now wait!" He held up both hands to keep his listeners from clamoring. "Since we're going, we might just as well be off this afternoon. Listen carefully, all of you." He spent several minutes relegating certain tasks to each person, then shouted in high excitement, like a cheer leader, "Come on now, everybody! Let's go!"

An hour later, Ponce and Gabe stood in their own ranch-yard with Desert Storm and the roan gelding, waiting for

David Forrest to guide the big covered truck down the lane and turn it around. When it halted, Joe Marino jumped down and, with Ponce helping, pulled out the long ramp and fitted it into place. The end-gates were swung wide, and Desert Storm and the roan were led up the ramp and tied in narrow stalls along with the five other horses from Shady Mesa.

With Ponce and Joe Marino riding with the horses, the big truck roared down the lane, turned onto the unpaved highway and sped west after Gil Dreen's pick-up, which held camping equipment and tools for constructing the corral. Five miles from the ranch, it bore down on the pick-up, and Gil Dreen stepped harder on the gas to stay in the lead. They followed the highway for fifty miles, then turned off onto a faint set of tracks which had been formed long ago by freight wagons carrying supplies to some mining boom town whose name had long since been forgotten. They made good time on the smooth, hard-packed sand. The thick cloud of dust they raised as they roared along hung suspended in the still air long after they had passed, as if determined to show that the peace and solitude of this great expanse of sand and sky had been disturbed, if only temporarily.

By three o'clock, they had reached their destination, a barren patch of sand and sagebrush close to the feet of the looming Mogollans. Again the ramp was run out and clamped into place, and one by one the seven horses were led out into the intense heat of afternoon. For the better part of an hour, Gabe was busy loading the pack horse which had been brought along, and his greatest difficulty consisted of keeping would-be helpers from undoing his work as fast as he did it. Eventually the animal was loaded, the racers and the roan were saddled, and Ponce started to lead out.

He turned for a final word. "We will travel a different way than the one taken by The Great Joto and me. It will be easier and shorter; but none of us must be careless. If any horse begins to tire, we will stop and rest."

He reined Desert Storm about and put her to an easy canter toward the break in the hills ahead. In an amazingly short time, they were winding up through the steep canyons and draws. Every now and then Ponce drew up to take his bearings from certain landmarks carefully described by The Old Apache. With his mind's eye, he retraced the map which Joto had drawn on the ground with a pointed stick before sending him off alone.

The riders threaded canyons, skirted cliffs and waterfalls and wound steadily up over long expanses of sandstone and granite. Twice they halted to water the horses and to rest them. The Forrest Thoroughbreds, unused to uneven ground and heavy stock saddles, burned up more energy fretting at the slowness of the pace than in actual work. The Iron Duke, under Joe Marino's expert handling, kept close on the heels of the black filly, doing his best to conceal his dislike for this country, which was obviously meant for mountain goats. The rangy chestnut filly was in a lather five minutes after setting forth. By the time the party climbed the last steep slope below the upland plain, she was played out.

Clattering up over the brow of the hill, Ponce rode out far enough to allow the others to come onto level ground. He sat looking across the plain toward the distant rock-walled valley of the wild gray stallion. He felt excitement begin to shake him as the others came up and exclaimed in hushed voices over the silent beauty of this lost wilderness. Then he rode toward the looming wall, picking out a group of figures standing around a low fire at the bottom of the trail.

Three young Apache men turned to stare at the cavalcade bearing down on them, and The Old Apache lifted a hand in solemn greeting. Ponce recognized the three bronze men as the ones who, with their women, had built Desert Storm's stable a year ago, and he smiled in their direction. Looking along the wall, he saw their horses grazing through the sage with The Old Apache's flea-bitten gray.

He drew up a little distance from the fire, letting the others of his party go on and dismount, with much animated talk and energetic handshaking. He sat quite still in the saddle, feeling excitement grip him at sight of the figures milling around. The hunters were assembled!

On the point of dismounting, he glanced up along the sheer face of the wall looming high above the now darkening plain. Nothing showed up there on the narrow ledge; but it seemed to him that two wicked black eyes were glaring down through the dusk. He felt those eyes fixed unwinkingly on him and saw in their glittering depths a question that was like an accusation hurled at him from that wind-swept ledge.

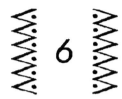

6

The Dangerous Game

FROM early light until deep dusk, the band of hunters worked at the foot of the valley's southern wall. Even Barbara refused to be considered a member of the weaker sex, for the time being, and labored with the men. Gabe and David Forrest alone were excused from this part of the expedition. Throughout the daylight hours these two kept to the high ledge and watched the movements of the little band of mares belonging to the gray stallion.

On the first morning of his stay, The Old Apache had gone to the foot of the inside trail and there left a patch torn from his blanket. After a single whiff of the hated man-smell, the gray had whirled and raced up the valley, driving his mares before him. They had swam the lake and had not again come into the lower half of the valley. Now the two older men watched them through strong field glasses, studying Victorio as he moved restlessly back and forth in the distance. Often they could see him on the edge of the lake, facing down wind, trying in vain to find an explanation for this danger that had come into his domain. And often he would send his scream of anger and fear down the wind, then whirl to race around the unscalable walls, searching for a way of escape which did not exist. If he ate at all, it was during the night hours.

While the hunters labored, erecting the corral in the south-western corner of the valley, the gray stallion never lowered his head to graze. Nor did he drink from the blue waters of the lake, behind which he had retreated. Hour after hour his uneasiness grew, until he could no longer stand motionless as he had done. He moved back and forth continually, his upflung head forever turned to the south where lay the danger he so strongly sensed but could neither see nor smell.

On the afternoon of the second day, The Old Apache moved along the eight-foot-high stockade, pushing and testing the thick pine logs set upright in the sand. He grunted in a satisfied way, when he could find no flaw in the construction. The logs had been sunk more than two feet into the ground and were lashed together midway up by ropes woven through them. At the top, long saplings were nailed for added strength. There were two of these walls. The other two sides of the corral were formed by the solid rock which towered high overhead. A narrow gate of stout poles closed the hundred-foot-square corral.

In one corner of the stockade, the three Apache men had constructed a strange looking affair known as a "bronco stall." Four posts were set deep in the ground. To them were bound eight-foot lengths of peeled logs, laid one on top of the other to a height of four feet. One end of the rectangular affair had been closed with four-foot logs. The whole thing measured eight feet by four and looked as if it could withstand the on-slaught of an angry elephant.

The Old Apache inspected it with great care. Finding it faultless, he went to the stout snubbing post in the middle of the corral and pushed at it. Since it was set four feet in the ground, he had no success in moving it. Nodding his approval one last time, he turned to his exhausted crew.

"We go now," he stated. "Tomorrow we see what we see."

The seven men and Barbara climbed out of the valley, descended to the plain . . . and tried to wait patiently for the day to end. When the sun sank behind the purple peaks, Gabe and David Forrest left their lookout and joined the others for the evening meal. Late into the night, The Old Apache talked beside the fire, telling each in turn what would be expected on the morrow. At last, there was silence along the foot of the mesa, except for the cry of the night wind over the empty plain and the steady rustle of the horses ranging through the sage in search of grass. The camp was asleep . . . all except Ponce.

Through the chill, dark hours, he lay in his blankets and watched the clouds scudding before the wind, high overhead. Knowing sleep to be impossible, he did not try; but kept his solitary vigil, attempting to picture the race that would take place at dawn. It had been described in detail by The Great Joto. Still—not even the all-seeing Apache could know everything that might occur when the giant-like gray stallion found himself pressed too closely by strange horses and by human beings whose very smell he hated. When the faint moonlight commenced to wane, the young Apache rose soundlessly and went out to bring in the horses.

Desert Storm and The Iron Duke were grazing side by side, some distance away. At his low call, they lifted their heads, nickered soft greetings and trotted up. Grasping the black filly's mane, Ponce vaulted astride and started for camp. One by one, the other grazing animals looked up, then charged after the black and the gray, as if terrified at the thought of being left behind. When they came to the foot of the trail leading up to the ledge, the whole camp was astir and waiting.

There was little conversation as each person claimed his mount and bridled it. Gabe, David Forrest, Gil Dreen and the three Apache men cinched heavy stock saddles on their mounts; but Ponce, Joe Marino and Barbara were to use nothing except the light racing bridles. There must be no unnecessary weight to slow the three thoroughbreds in the coming race.

It still lacked a good hour before full daylight as the party mounted and filed up the narrow trail, crossed the ledge and descended to the valley. Between the walls, the narrow plain was drowned in chill gloom, and little tendrils of mist drifted along close to the ground, swept before the wind from the lake.

The Old Apache rode a short distance out into the grass and halted. When Ponce, Joe Marino and Barbara drifted up, he spoke to them briefly.

"Victorio stays close to the far wall, until the sun puts warmth into this place. With the wind thus, he will see and smell nothing until you, Joe Marino, are upon him. Take off your shirt and, if he charges you, wave it. He will not come close. Keep as near to him as you can. Barbara, when you ride out, be certain he sees you, else he may think a foolish mare dares to chase him and turn on your filly."

He hesitated, peering through the gloom and mist at Ponce. "Your heart has a softness!" he said harshly in Apache. "Harden it, when the time comes, or a bad thing will happen. Know you that!" He lifted a skinny arm to the north. "Go you now."

In a straight line, the three Thoroughbreds went up the valley, their hoofs making practically no sound on the spongy turf. It was distinctly cold at this high altitude, with the previous day's heat sucked out of the ground and the rocks by the night wind. Traveling the five miles to the lake at a swinging canter, the three horses were barely warmed up.

At the edge of the lake, Joe Marino and Barbara hesitated only a moment before putting their reluctant mounts into the cold waters. The Iron Duke obeyed Joe Marino's command with but little show of uneasiness; but Last Laugh reared and tried to turn, until Barbara struck her with the crop dangling from her wrist. The chestnut plunged through the shallow water for a hundred feet, then dropped suddenly out of sight, to reappear a moment later, coughing and blowing. She gave no more trouble; but swam strongly after the gray colt.

Ponce waited until the others had struck the shelving bank on the far side before turning Desert Storm and walking her back along the pines below the wall. For ten minutes he kept up the warming exercise, feeling her grow increasingly restive as her muscles loosened. She tossed her head constantly and danced along sideways. Tension was building up in her. From the instant she had glimpsed Ponce this morning, she had sensed excitement in the air, and her nerves had tightened until she was half crazy with the urge to run.

Starting to turn at the end of the exercise ground he had chosen, Ponce glimpsed a narrow opening in the pines to his left. He looked closer, saw where a section of the wall had crumbled and fallen down to form a high knoll whose top was almost level with the tops of the trees. He turned quickly into the pines. A moment later, he was atop the knoll and looking out over the trees toward the upper end of the valley. It was growing lighter now, and in the thin air at this altitude, distant objects loomed startlingly close.

Once he thought he detected a faint movement of color along the upper end of the valley; but he could not be certain. Of Barbara and Joe Marino there was no sign. The girl, he knew, would by now be in her place, halfway along the course that had been set. Joe Marino was, in all probability, threading his way through the pines. It was more than likely that he had reached the far end, where the small band of wild horses were known to be at this early hour.

Despairing of seeing anything from this distance, Ponce descended to level ground and again moved Desert Storm back and forth to keep her loosened up. He did not know how long he had been at that task, when some inner sense made him whirl the big black and again climb the knoll. His breath stopped in his throat at the sight before him.

A speck of color was moving swiftly down the middle of the valley, coming out of the shadow of the high wall into full light. Ponce watched it come on, grow more distinct, and he knew that it was the band of eight mares in full flight. They swept along in a tight-pressed bunch, trying to keep ahead of the giant gray that swept back and forth at their rear, like a darting, threatening shadow. They had come two miles at that high speed, and it was obvious some of them were beginning to tire. Time and again one of them would veer out, trying to escape; but always the streaking gray anticipated the move and bore in to close up the ranks.

For two endless minutes, Ponce watched the wild race. Twice he saw the gray stallion halt and whirl to gaze back over the way he had come. When this happened a third time, Ponce saw the reason for it. Coming steadily down on the fleeing band was Joe Marino on The Iron Duke. The magnificent Kentucky Derby winner was still far behind; but he was beginning to move faster with every stride of his long, flashing legs.

"Come on, Iron Duke!" Ponce shouted wildly. "Come *on!*"

A half mile to the rear of his quarry, the tall Thoroughbred flattened his sleek body nearer to the ground and went into his sprint. He closed in with startling swiftness, running with that wonderful, floating action of his. It was clear that the clever Joe Marino had been saving him for this last stretch drive.

For the space of a dozen heartbeats, the wild gray stood with head upflung, watching the Thoroughbred streaking down on him. Then he whirled and sped after the slowing mares at a speed that left Ponce dazed. The stallion's black-stockinged legs were an invisible blur against the dark ground as he lined out in that dazzling rush. He appeared to float just off the ground, without visible motion or effort. Coming up on the mares, he was forced to slow. For another quarter mile he ran behind them, his head turned back over his shoulder as he watched that other gray move remorselessly up.

Yard by yard, The Iron Duke closed in. For a hundred yards more the band stayed ahead of him, then Joe Marino's left arm commenced to rise and fall in steady rhythm, as the jockey took to the whip. The racer responded with a final burst of speed, sweeping in to press the stallion still closer. And Victorio, terrified and puzzled, abandoned his mares. He went through their ranks, scattering them like quail, and set himself to outrun the now tiring Iron Duke.

For another hundred yards the Thoroughbred held to the chase; but when a movement off to the left told Joe Marino that Barbara was ready to play her part, he pulled the exhausted colt in. He waved a hand, slowed to a canter, and watched David Forrest's $40,000 chestnut filly start her move against Victorio.

Ponce had seen Last Laugh run but a few times. Now he

fully realized how well-grounded were Gil Dreen's boasts about the filly's speed. She came away from the pines at an angle and took out after the gray stallion like a frightened bird. For a brief time only she seemed unsure of herself, going with head high and tail twisted up over her rump. But within a hundred yards she had found her stride and settled.

A half mile flashed behind frantically drumming hoofs. Clearly it was not necessary for Barbara to show herself, for the big stallion took only one glance at this new threat before facing ahead again and throwing himself into panicked flight. At first he pulled away from the furiously running chestnut; but after a half mile he ceased to gain.

Seeing that, Ponce experienced a flash of doubt that gradually changed to disappointment. The gray stallion was not proving himself to be the great racer the Apache boy had expected. True, he had already run over four miles at high speed. In all likelihood, he had scarcely eaten or drunk for over three days, and the fast could not fail to affect his stamina. Still, he was somehow losing stature in the young man's eyes. And then disappointment and doubt died in Ponce as he continued to watch the race going on down there.

The chestnut filly had ceased to gain. Traveling at the peak of her speed, she had come up to within a hundred feet of the stallion. But there she hung as Victorio, without visible effort, lengthened his strides just enough to maintain that distance between him and his pursuer. Barbara moved her heels demandingly against the chestnut barrel; three times she tapped the churning shoulders with her crop, signaling for more speed. Last Laugh responded with everything she had. It was not enough. Try as she might, she could not cut more precious feet from that gap. She held on for the better part of a mile, twice veering out to head Victorio off as he sought to go wide of the lake. When the blue waters rose in a glinting spray before the stallion's chest and flailing hoofs, she was still a hundred feet to the rear.

From the knoll, Ponce watched Barbara bring the chestnut up to the edge of the lake. The gray was swimming swiftly, pointing for the opposite shore. Then, even as the girl hesitated, that wicked head veered toward the right side of the lake. Ponce darted a look at Barbara, sensing what she would do. He gasped, then shouted a warning that was never heard as the chestnut plunged into the water under her rider's stern handling. The next instant the Apache had whirled Desert Storm off the knoll and was crashing down through the trees. He knew all too well that the girl would force Victorio to swim in a straight line, whatever the danger and the cost might be.

He pulled Desert Storm to a halt at the edge of the trees and waited . . . waited with his breath stopped in his throat and with his heart hammering wildly against his ribs.

But Barbara's plan proved successful. With the chestnut filly and the hated human figure behind him, the stallion abandoned all attempts to swing to the right and concentrated on gaining the far shore. He swam strongly, plowing through the blue water without visible effort. Only his head was above water, so that his feet never broke the surface, and that head revolved constantly as the staring eyes sought a way of escape from the unfamiliar danger closing in. Ponce gazed at the finely chiseled head in morbid fascination. It reminded him of a snake he had once seen swimming across the arroyo in flood season. But whereas the serpent had moved silently and unseeingly, the stallion's red-rimmed nostrils bespoke the terror which drove him. In evenly-spaced bursts of sound, that terror rasped from gaping mouth and nostrils, while the red-flecked eyes blazed steadily out from beneath the dripping forelock.

Ponce was seized by a numbing chill . . . and guilt. What greed had made him seek to rob this magnificent creature of its freedom? What right had he to commit such a crime? He would not—could not be the one to ride the gray down—not after witnessing that heartbreaking struggle for freedom. He

gasped for breath. His mouth felt hot and dry. He must signal Barbara to turn back. In that instant, he heard a voice echoing and reechoing in the silence of the long valley.

"Your heart has a softness! Harden it, when the time comes, or a bad thing will happen!"

The gray head came on. The striking hoofs found the shelving bottom of the lake. The gleaming body heaved up out of the deep water into the shallows and plunged toward him. And still the head turned back and forth, seeking . . . seeking.

Horror gripped Ponce as he realized finally what the bad thing was.

Victorio came through the shallows and out of them in a foaming cascade of spray and gravel. For a moment he poised on the edge of the lake, facing down the valley, his head held high on the muscle-corded neck as he tested the wind and sought to pierce the distance with his eyes. Behind him, the chestnut filly came on, nearing the shallows. And behind him, as if to put an end to the awful suspense, Barbara's voice sounded.

The stallion quivered. His ears went flat. He rose on his hind legs, emitting a terrifying scream as he whirled and came down facing the lake. He tensed there, sinking into a crouch, like a tawny mountain cat. Water ran off his heaving flanks. The sound of his labored breathing was like muted thunder in the silence of the valley. Legs wide set under him, his head snaked forward, he waited. His eyes were fixed un-winkingly on the girl coming steadily toward him on the chestnut. *And there was murder in them.*

7

The Strength of Terror

WITH a ringing cry, Ponce flung Desert Storm away from the trees, straight at the threatening creature at the water's edge. For a single shocked instant Victorio stood rooted in his tracks, his head darting around, his glazed eyes taking in the picture of the black rushing down upon him. For that endless instant it seemed that he would spring to meet the filly's charge. Then, with a scream of hopeless rage and fear, he whirled and streaked down the valley, his wet body flashing in the strengthening light.

Desert Storm went after him like a coursing greyhound. Within two hundred feet, she was reaching for her top stride and beginning to close in with amazing swiftness. Her long legs strode out, retracted, reached again, like the limbs of a giant, hurling her onward ever faster. Pressed flat along her neck, Ponce felt those lengthening strides. He urged her sharply for a quarter mile, then glanced to the front. A grim smile touched his lips when he saw that Victorio was unable to outdistance her.

Those dark legs of the stallion's were, he knew, a trifle longer than the filly's. Throughout the race with The Iron Duke, then out in front of Last Laugh, they had worked like perfectly-timed pistons, holding the stallion safely out of reach of the hunters. But strain as he might, he could not now add one yard to his 200-foot lead. Remembering how he had moved with The Iron Duke challenging him, Ponce knew that he was tiring at last.

He had run over five miles at close to top speed. He could not hold himself to that smooth, floating action any longer. He was visibly laboring as he fought to stave off this latest threat. In less than a mile, he began to fall back, foot by foot, as the filly, fresh and crazy to run, thundered along his trail. The distance separating them closed to less than a hundred feet. For another half mile, then, Ponce rated Desert Storm, gauging the manner of the stallion's going, waiting for the undeniable break in those reaching strides that would foretell defeat. He concentrated his attention on the streaming silver tail, knowing that it would be the first to betray Victorio's exhaustion. Moments before, it had floated out high and straight back from the heaving rump. It was sinking now, beginning to describe a whipping, circular motion. And as the race held, it whipped harder and harder, erasing all doubt. The stallion was at the end of his endurance.

Half blinded by the wind and the filly's slashing mane, Ponce kept his gaze fixed on the fleeing gray. He was less than fifty feet behind him now, going steadily up, pressing him mercilessly. The sound of the racing hoofs was like dulled heartbeats on the springy turf, the sound of the stallion's agonized breathing like choking sobs. And with that awful sound in his ears, Ponce felt his heart swell within him until it seemed that it must burst. Never before had he experienced such admiration and awe for a horse. The feeling of guilt he had known back at the lake was gone altogether as foot by foot he brought Desert Storm up. For the first time in his life he fully understood the meaning of the oft-voiced phrase, "the heart of a Thoroughbred." Except that his own eyes told him the truth, he would not have believed that any animal could have withstood the pressure thrown against it that Victorio had with-

stood this day. He released his grip on Desert Storm's reins, overpowered by the desire to come up on Victorio and capture him before that great heart burst.

The filly shot ahead, as if propelled by invisible springs. Low to the ground, she fled in that dazzling, heart-stopping action that had brought thousands of racing fans to their feet in hysterical applause. And the stallion, fighting with deadened legs and empty lungs, could not hold her off.

She drew alongside, edged against him, matched him stride for stride. But from some bottomless well, the terrified gray summoned up the last dregs of his stamina. For fifty yards more he ran on with the strength and the courage of desperation. It was no good. Despite the valiant effort, he was defeated by the big filly, who clung to his side like a leech and pressed him steadily.

In Victorio there was no thought of turning aside, no thought of striking out with hoof and teeth, no thought of winning his freedom. Side by side, the two animals thundered down the valley, and now they looked like two grays. From muzzle to croup the black was covered with foamy lather. On the deeply cushioned grass, they made practically no sound. Like two ghosts from the spirit world, they raced side by side for the looming wall in the distance.

Ponce centered every nerve of his being on the final part he must play in this frightful game. He uncoiled the length of braided rawhide from about his waist and shook the loop out wider. Under him, the filly's body was slick with lather, and when he bent his left leg beneath him and tried to rest the instep across the backbone, it slipped repeatedly. Four times he attempted to get it in place and failed. The fifth time, he succeeded. With the wind a deafening roar in his ears, with his eyes streaming, he glanced aside and picked out the section of the gray's whipping mane which he must grasp. Slowly he leaned out.

In his palm the coarse mane was like a mass of coiling wires. He clenched his fingers until the nails cut into his palm, and, as the two animals ran on, he straightened his left leg, lifted himself into the air and felt himself falling sideways into space. He writhed in mid-air, throwing his right leg out. Victorio stumbled, crashed against Desert Storm, then veered away. In that instance Ponce was jerked astride the stallion.

For the first time in his life, the Apache boy knew stark, numbing terror. He could not get a grip with his thighs. Victorio's action was utterly different from the filly's, savagely jarring, broken from exhaustion. The bulging muscles which can so easily lift a stallion on his hind legs, writhed and bunched under him like live things. The boy felt himself slipping to the left and grabbed the thick mane with both hands. Victorio stumbled again, and Ponce slipped far to the right. Again he fought to keep his seat.

Twice he threw the looped rawhide. Twice it whipped back. The third time, the circle fell over the outthrust muzzle, and the boy drew it tight. Only then did he become aware that Desert Storm was no longer alongside. Out of the corner of his eye, he glimpsed her cantering off at an angle, aiming toward the pines, her head held high and to one side, to avoid the trailing reins.

Ponce faced forward, warned by Victorio's shifting action. The stallion was still running; but his strides were breaking. He went on another hundred yards, then plunged to a halt.

The Apache had expected that. Before the stallion could collect himself, the braided rawhide popped against his lathered rump with a noise like a gunshot. The pliant reata inflicted no pain upon the thick, dappled hide; but the noise it made in striking startled the stallion. He reared, shrieking and flailing the air with his forefeet. The reata popped against his shoulder, and he came down and switched ends, like a snapped whip. He bucked once, then reared again. For a moment he stood motionless, poised like a terrible shadow, then, with a strangled scream, he flung himself over backwards, seeking to crush his tormentor beneath his great weight.

Ponce had expected that also. He rolled to the left, freeing himself, as the stallion crashed to earth. Before the half-dazed animal had again regained his feet, he was once more astride.

Insane with rage and terror, Victorio bellowed and bucked in a tight circle. As he reared a third time, the reata popped against his neck. He came down on all fours and fled toward the wall and the remembered trail. Twice he skidded to a halt and sought to dislodge the rider from his back, and twice the popping reata frightened him into labored flight. A fourth time he halted; but this time he stood quivering on wide-spread legs, unable to struggle further. When Ponce urged him onward with heels and rope, he quivered again, then plodded ahead, his muzzle scant inches above the grass that was still jeweled with the morning dew.

The grueling race and battle had not left Ponce unmarked. The fall had bruised him and torn a long gash across his bare chest. Both hands were bloody from gripping the reata and fighting Victorio's head up. From head to foot he was covered with blood-flecked foam, and he reeled dazedly atop the staggering stallion.

The horsemen, waiting at the foot of the wall, raced forward, Gabe Stuart in the lead. The old rancher dashed up, swinging his lasso in a wide circle over his head. He shouted to Ponce; but the youth gave no sign that he heard.

The roan gelding wheeled and dodged in close. "Get off him, son!" Gabe yelled. "I'm goin' to rope him. GET OFF!"

Ponce tried to answer, tried to call out; but his bruised lips would not move. He could only shake his head numbly. It was one of the young Apache men who realized that he could neither speak nor move. He circled the stallion on his stocky bay, then sent it in close. The man's arm flashed out in the sun, lifting Ponce and holding him firmly as the bay wheeled and galloped off a hundred feet. The Apache rider drew up, threw a leg over the horn and slid to the ground. He lowered Ponce into the grass. For one brief instant the man looked down into Ponce's eyes, a slow smile moving across his face.

"Good man," he said in guttural tones. "I call you brother now."

The bay wheeled, and a moment later two singing loops flashed out and dropped over the gray stallion's lowered head. What followed left everyone gasping in astonishment.

The low-swinging head jerked up at the tightening sensation about the thick neck, and the dark eyes were again aflame with the lust to kill. For the fraction of a second Victorio froze in his tracks, then, with a strangled scream, he darted his head around, his long yellow teeth gleaming in the sunlight. There was a sharp, metallic click, and Gabe Stuart's lasso dropped into the dust, cleanly cut two feet from the bulging neck. Someone shouted a warning; but it came too late.

Like a striking snake, the gray stallion whipped about and propelled himself straight at the Apache whose rope held him. The man yelled and jumped his bay around, trying to escape;

but the stallion swerved in mid-stride and struck the stocky pony like a battering ram. The pony crashed down, its legs flailing wildly, and Victorio hurtled on over the fallen horse and rider. He took three jumps before he hit the end of the lasso, which was still secured to the saddle of the downed pony. The rope popped like a gunshot, and Victorio was thrown end over end, to strike the ground with a force that could be felt a hundred yards away. His breath went out of him in a loud explosion; but even as he fell, he writhed around and was instantly on his feet. He pivoted to flee, but the rope held, and the bay, just rising to its feet, was jerked down and dragged by the bellowing, lunging gray.

Like a great cat, Victorio twisted and leaped and fought to rid himself of that choking loop of fire about his throat. Again and again his rage and terror burst from his gaping mouth in deafening shrieks that seemed to fill all the valley. For fifty feet he dragged the helplessly struggling bay, whose rider could do nothing except follow along and make futile grabs at the firmly tied lasso. Then he whirled and rushed the pony a second time.

There was then an endless moment in which shrieking, milling horses and riders and a thick cloud of dust numbed the senses. The second and third Apache riders flashed in between the stallion and the fallen pony, their ropes twirling about their heads. And Gabe Stuart, his second lasso in his hand, ran his gelding around behind, trying for another throw.

Suddenly all action ceased. The dust drifted to the earth, and Victorio stood on widely-braced legs, helpless and defeated. Four taut ropes extended from his neck to the saddle horns of Gabe and the three Apaches, and he could not move an inch in any direction. His eyes glazed and became set in his mud-caked head. The sound of his breathing was like the roaring of the wind across the mountains.

Ponce lifted himself on his elbows and lay watching the sickening scene. He had not believed any animal was capable of displaying such naked, murderous rage and fear and strength. Dimly he remembered stories of wild stallions which had chosen death rather than submit to capture at the hands of man, and he knew that Victorio was one of those. He watched the senseless struggle go on and on, until it seemed it would never stop until the gray stallion lay dead on the ground. Dimly he heard himself shouting to the Apache who had dismounted and was inching his way along one of the ropes.

"Quickly, my brother! Oh, go quickly! He will die!"

The man gave no sign that he had heard; but continued his slow progress, his glittering eyes never leaving the eyes of Victorio. From them would come the danger signals.

In the man's hand was a four-foot length of cotton rope. He trailed it along at his side, now and then flipping it to make certain it was still straight. He went on until three feet lay between him and the trembling, heaving stallion; then he moved forward another six inches. For a long moment he stood there, staring into the blazing eyes, then his hand that held the length of rope flicked out, like a striking snake. The end of the rope flipped around behind the widely-spread forelegs and was caught by the Apache. An instant later, the noose lay against one of Victorio's pasterns. The Apache stepped back, his shoulder muscles bunching. He jerked hard, tightening the noose, and as Victorio made one last frantic lunge, his legs buckled under him, and he crashed to the ground.

Too swiftly for the eye to follow, the Apache darted in, grabbed the flailing hind legs, took a series of half turns with the rope and stepped back.

Sick with dismay, Ponce pushed himself to his feet and staggered over. For a moment he stood staring down at the great animal whose defeat he had brought about. Then he felt himself falling forward into whirling, roaring blackness.

8

"He Is a Killer!"

FOR a half hour the shaken hunters stood in a circle about the helpless stallion, even now not quite trusting that he would stay bound. They had witnessed too much nerve-shattering excitement in the closing moments of the deadly struggle to breathe easily until the bloody, gasping, lathered demon was safely barred inside the stout corral.

They all turned to watch in silence as Barbara and Joe Marino came up on their exhausted racers. A hundred feet away, Barbara saw the stallion lying helpless in their midst and kicked Last Laugh into a gallop. She slid to the ground, ran in close—and burst into tears.

"Oh, Dad!" she cried, "What have we done?"

David Forrest could not speak. He went over, put a comforting arm about the shaking shoulders and pulled the brown head close against his chest. After a long moment he said gently, "It's all right, honey. It's all right."

"But it's not!" Barbara cried, pushing away and turning wide eyes to her father's face. "He earned his freedom! He outran The Iron Duke! Last Laugh couldn't catch him!" She whirled, pointing an accusing finger at Desert Storm, who had come in and now stood nearby. "And *she* couldn't have caught him either, if it had been an equal race!"

"Honey! Honey!" David Forrest said soothingly. "You mustn't go on like this. Now let's . . ."

Barbara's voice rose to a shrill shriek. "I don't *care!* It's not right, what we've done! You've got to turn him . . ."

Her words ended abruptly as her father held her at arm's length and shook her ungently. "Barbara!" he said sharply. "That will be enough!" He paused, then spoke in a calmer tone. "Now listen to me very carefully. You saw Victorio at his best—in full flight, running free—and for you the whole thing, the running down business, was just a game. You didn't think ahead to the *end* of the race, nor think of *why* we might be doing this.

"I readily admit it's a sad scene, right now. I don't blame you for crying. Whenever I read of a criminal being sent to prison, I feel somehow sorry for him, because he will not be able to walk about freely any more, nor smell the breezes, nor feel the sun on his face. But I don't say he should be left free to commit more crimes! If he has it in him, he will become a good, useful citizen while he's in prison. He will have every opportunity to learn a useful trade. It's up to him.

"Victorio is a criminal." When Barbara started to speak, he demanded in a louder tone, "Where do you think he got those eight mares? I'll tell you. Every one of them belongs to some rancher from whose pasture Victorio stole her. I haven't had a chance to get a good look at this stud's teeth; but I'm willing to bet he's not over four years old. That means he has stolen an average of two mares a year; but he didn't start stealing until he was at least two—which means he has averaged *four* mares a year! Is it fair to ranchers to let this wild stud go on stealing their finest brood-stock? How would *you* feel, if you went out to bring Last Laugh in from her paddock some morning, only to find *her* gone? $40,000 *gone!*"

There was a long silence. Everyone was thinking about what the horseman had just said and realizing the truth in it. Barbara was an intelligent girl, and though her heart ached for the pitiful-looking gray stallion lying in the dust nearby, she would not hold to a position which had been proven to be a wrong one.

"Dad," she said quietly, "I'm sorry. I never thought . . . It's just that he looks so frightened and helpless."

Her father drew her back into the curve of his arm. "Of course he does, honey. But we'll start thinking of him as if he were a criminal, which he is. And we'll start hoping that in prison he will learn how to become an upright, useful citizen. Right?"

"Right!" Barbara said, and joined in the relieved laughter that ran around the circle.

Joe Marino had come up in time to hear most of his employer's lecture. When everyone laughed, he jumped down from the beaten Iron Duke and walked over to examine the wild stallion at close range. His dark eyes got wider and wider, the longer he looked, and he made a shrill whistling noise in his throat.

"Goll-eeee!" he muttered, taking in the points of the captive. "Talk about a *horse!* What he couldn't do to a track couldn't be *done!*" He broke off, catching sight of Ponce lying in the grass, a dozen yards away. "What's wrong with him?"

Gabe Stuart was squatting beside the unconscious young man, bathing the scratched and bruised face with his handkerchief, which he had wet from a canteen. He said briefly, "Passed out; but he's all right. Little too much horse for one day, I reckon."

The jockey was beside him before he had finished speaking; but, quick as he was, Barbara was before him. They knelt, staring down into the battered, pale face. One eye was swollen shut from a wide, purplish bruise. The full lips were faintly blue, and the lower one bore deep tooth marks. The naked upper part of Ponce's body contained countless cuts and bruises. One wide skid burn showed angrily red against the bronze skin of his left side. Barbara burst into tears again.

Joe Marino rose to his feet and stepped away. "Poor kid," he muttered, shaking his curly head. "I'll make no bones about statin' that I'd sooner tackle a wildcat barehanded than that gray devil! Wow! Can he ever tear up the turf!"

David Forrest, who had until now resisted the temptation to ask about the earlier part of the race, could contain himself no longer. "How'd it go, Joe?" he questioned. "Did The Duke give him a run?"

"Ha!" the jockey snorted. "The Duke and I were never *in* the race! First time in his life I ever knew that colt to want to do something besides run."

"What do you mean?" David Forrest demanded, coming close. "You're not going to try to tell us he wanted to *fight*?"

Joe Marino's eyes were twinkling. He was getting a great kick out of watching Shady Mesa's owner tottering on the verge of a breakdown of his usual control. He rubbed his black, short hair. "Well," he drawled, "he didn't exactly *say* that was what he had in mind, but I kinda gathered as much, from certain little hints he gave me, such as trying to bounce me onto the ground, standin' up on his hind legs an' makin' like a trick-dog, an' all but turnin' flips. You know, that crazy colt up an' tried to *buck* me off? Yipee! I'll have nightmares about this for a month!"

By now, Gil Dreen was practically jumping up and down with impatience. "Joe!" he shouted. "Will you tell us what *happened*? Never mind your dreams!"

Joe Marino grinned hugely. "Well, sure," he said in a surprised voice. "Why didn't you *say* you wanted to know? Well, The Duke, here, started pawin' up sod an' bellerin' like a mad bull the minute he caught sight of the gray stud. After about a minute of makin' like a bronc buster,* I figured I'd best do what Joto told me to, an' do it quick! I yanked off my shirt an' took off after the bunch that had strung out

* A rider of wild horses. The nick name "Bronco Buster" is most commonly applied to rodeo riders today.

in a dead run, with the gray workin' 'em over right an' left, to make sure they kept their mind on runnin'. Only trouble was, I couldn't get The Duke's mind on that little piece of business. He kept tryin' to get rid of me, until I worked him over a little. By then, though, we were almost a mile behind the wild bunch.

"I finally got The Duke lined out; but it was too late to do much chasin', so I figured I might as well give old Dukie his mornin' work out. We started coastin' right along, then. The mares were gettin' tired of all this foolishness an' kept tryin' to break away, so they could stop. They didn't argue one tiny little bit, though, when the gray showed what pretty teeth he had. Still, two miles just about did them in. That was when I started shootin' ducks an' whoop-dee-doin'-it for home."

"Started *what*?" Gabe exclaimed. "What in tarnation you talkin' about, boy. Shootin' ducks an' what?"

David Forrest explained, smilingly. "Whoop-dee-doin'-it for home is track slang meaning to turn a racer loose and ask him to give every ounce of speed he's got."

"Oh," Gabe muttered. "I—Well, go on, Joe."

The jockey obviously enjoyed his role of story-teller. He nodded quickly and plunged back into the story. "Didn't take us long to come up on the mares, of course; an' we went through them like a couple of jet fighters. The Duke made up his mind he was goin' to catch the other stud, an' for a minute there I thought he just might. He was pickin' 'em up an' layin' 'em down like a hound dog after a jackrabbit; but he couldn't do any better than hold his place for a couple hundred yards. He *did* hold on that long; but by then he'd run more than his distance, an' when Barbara came out of the pines like a scared antelope on Last Laugh, I eased The Duke in. Gosh, he was mad!"

David Forrest turned and called to Barbara. "Honey, come over here an' tell us how your part went!"

She rose from Ponce's side and walked over. "There's not much to add," she said. "I heard Joe telling you about The Duke. You know, when he started closing in, I almost collapsed. It looked as if he was going to catch Victorio! Then, I saw he wasn't going to make it, so I got ready. At first I couldn't get that silly Last Laugh lined out. She was running off the ground* for a hundred yards; but I gave her a good whack and she settled down. The whip made her mad, and she took off as if she had no doubt whatsoever about catching the stud. The farther she went, the madder she got. You know, I really believe she'd have tried to knock him to pieces, if she'd caught him!"

She paused and turned to her father. "Dad, you certainly didn't throw your money away when you bought her. She's going to sweep everything you put her in this winter. I know that! She didn't sweep the gray stud, though. At the top of her sprint, she started closing in. She got within a hundred feet of him; but then I saw that he had let her do that. She poured it on for over a mile; but she couldn't do it. Twice I had to take her out to keep the stud headed for the lake, and when he was in the water, he started to turn, so I put Last Laugh in after him."

She stopped and, with her father's eyes steady on her, suddenly dropped her gaze to the ground.

"Go on, Barbara," said David Forrest. "There's something else, isn't there? What happened?"

"I . . . well . . . I . . ."

"We're waiting, Barbara," urged her father.

For a long moment Barbara continued staring at the ground, then she drew a long breath, expelled it quickly and looked up. "I don't think I ought to say this, because it probably

---

* An expression common in racing circles, meaning that a horse is moving with high, exaggerated action, instead of reaching out in long, full strides. It occurs most frequently at the start of a race, and can spell the difference between defeat and victory, unless corrected instantly.

doesn't mean a thing. I don't know anything about wild studs; they probably all act that way."

"What way, Barbara?" her father asked gently.

"Well, Victorio *turned*, when he hit dry land. Last Laugh and I were still about fifty feet from him, when he whirled and stood there, glaring at us like an insane monster. I never saw a horse look like that before. He seemed ready to jump at us, the minute we came within reach."

"*What happened?*"

David Forrest's shout startled Barbara so that she jumped. "Ponce came out on Desert Storm," she said quickly. "He was yelling at the top of his voice, and it scared Victorio, and he turned and ran. You know the rest."

There was a stunned silence for a full minute after the girl finished her recital. David Forrest stood looking straight before him. He breathed long and slowly, then let the air run out in a thin thread of sound. "Thank you, God," he whispered. His eyes swung to Gil Dreen, and the two exchanged a long, slow look of understanding. He said nothing more, but he began to shake his head slowly from side to side, as if waking from a horrible nightmare.

No one had taken any notice of The Old Apache during the telling of the two stories. All this while he had been squatting cross-legged on the ground, less than a dozen feet from the bound gray stallion. In that time his eyes had never ceased to study the animal. While the voices had gone on rising and falling behind him, he had steadily gazed into Victorio's dark orbs, searching for something he seemed to know was there, but which he could not find. His hands lay flat across his thighs, and he was bent slightly forward. He appeared wholly at ease, wholly relaxed. His black eyes showed no expression other than one of vague puzzlement. The thing that gave him away to Ponce, when the Apache boy regained consciousness, was his complete deafness to his, Ponce's question.

"What is it, my father?" the youth asked. "What do you see?"

He rose, wincing with pain, and came halfway to the motionless Joto, then stopped, knowing he must not break in upon the ancient warrior's concentration. Swaying slightly, he stood in the bright glare of the sun and watched that silent, intent probing go on and on. And as he watched, he felt something dark and sinister hovering between the stallion and the warrior. A chill shook him, though perspiration was standing out on his exposed skin. Almost against his will he asked again, "What is it, my father? What do you see?" Then he clenched his teeth against further sound. Trembling, he waited for the break to come. Without turning his eyes away, he knew that everyone else was staring at The Old Apache.

The break came with surprising suddenness. One instant, The Old Apache was locked behind the dark doors of his thoughts. The next instant, he was on his feet and facing the others. He addressed the three Apache riders in a quiet, matter-of-fact tone.

"Delgadito, take you the hackamore you have made ready. Juan, go you behind Victorio and grasp with your teeth one of his ears. You know how it is done. Dallo Chie, go you with Delgadito. Move with him, and as he holds the hackamore ready, grasp you with your fingers Victorio's nostrils. Do this quickly, and without fear. He tells me he will not fight; but I know not whether to believe him."

He said this last so casually that for an instant no one realized the significance of the words. When they did, they exchanged startled glances, then turned back as the three Apaches moved in on Victorio.

Like men who knew their business, the lithe riders went in behind the stallion. For a moment they paused, then a silent signal passed among them, and they darted forward like bronze shadows, their arms reaching for Victorio's motionless head. Juan's teeth flashed whitely, then clamped over one

pointed ear in a twisting, grinding hold.* Dallo Chie, moving
with him, reached out and fastened the fingers of both hands
into the flared nostrils. Caught between the two vice-like,
agonizing holds, the stallion uttered a single, startled groan,
then froze.

Coming in around the crouching Dallo Chie, Delgadito
knelt and waited until the other released the delicate muzzle.
With a single, darting motion, he slipped the hackamore on,
then slid around close to Juan and waited until Dallo Chie
again had the nostrils clenched between his fingers. Juan released the ear, and Delgadito looped the hackamore around
the top of the head and secured it under the jaw with a series
of tightly-drawn knots. Again an unvoiced signal ran between
Dallo Chie and Delgadito. They moved back in a long jump,
and Victorio lay on his side, the hackamore firmly fitted to
his head.

Throughout the painful process, he had made no move to
resist.

The Old Apache grunted shortly. "Ah, so," he said softly.
"He did not lie . . . that time. We will see if he spoke truly
of the other matter."

Again the white watchers exchanged startled glances, then
moved quickly back, as The Old Apache waved them to a
greater distance. He picked up the long rope attached to the
hackamore. "Dallo Chie," he said quietly, "bring to me the
whip from my horse." While the young man moved to obey,
he stood gazing into the stallion's eyes. He turned to face the
group, as a low gasp rose from them at the sight of the whip.

It was of braided rawhide, twelve feet in length, with a
heavy stock which tapered into the narrow lash. At the end of
the lash three smaller lashes were attached. These were six
inches long and were made of rawhide rolled to the thinness

* This is a technique known as "Earing down." Though painful to the horse,
it is most effective, and often the sole means of holding a particularly vicious
animal still.

of heavy wire while still wet. Dry, they were as hard as wire, though more flexible. In the hands of an expert, they could flay the skin from an animal . . . or a man. In Joto's hand, it resembled a deadly snake with out-thrust fangs. Even motionless, it was a thing of cruelty.

The Old Apache flipped his wrist slightly, and the repulsive goad writhed off the ground, its distant end looping, then straightening. The wire-like lashes flicked out and rested across the stallion's shoulders; but the animal did not move so much as a muscle.

The Old Apache was all the while watching the faces of his little audience. "Did he move?" he asked softly, and there was the shadow of a smile hovering around his deepset eyes. When every head shook in denial, he spoke again in the same soft voice. "Is it not strange he did not move? Is it not natural for a wild thing to fear any new thing? Yet Victorio shows no fear of this cruel lash." He paused, moving his white head up and down. "Yes," he went on. "It is cruel. You are right. It is very, very cruel. It could kill. It can cut the flesh from a horse as easily as can a knife. I made it carefully, and perhaps you will understand why in a very little while."

He turned back to the stallion and spoke to Ponce without looking at him. "Let him up, my son. Untie the rope that binds his feet. Do it without fear. He will not harm you."

Ponce moved forward, his eyes fixed on the gray giant who lay as still as a stone. He was within two yards of the extended legs when Barbara darted in front of him.

"No!" she cried in terror. "You must not do it, Ponce! He will kill you!"

The Old Apache's voice reached out like a heavy hand and whirled her around. "Get you gone! There is no danger!"

Barbara held her ground, staring back at Joto defiantly. "But . . ." she began.

Her father's voice cut off her words. "Barbara," he called

sternly, "come over here immediately. He knows what he's doing."

"But . . ." Barbara repeated.

"I said *come over here!*" David Forrest said loudly. "If this is the way you're going to act, you will stay home next time!"

The girl looked at Ponce, then at her father. Without further protest, she stepped aside and returned to her place between her father and Gil Dreen.

Ponce took two steps, bent and commenced to work at the tight knots. They did not come undone easily, and during the time he crouched close to Victorio, he could feel the heat rise from the stallion like air from a furnace. Twice he glanced up, but Victorio's head never moved. For all the attention he payed the youth, the animal might have been completely alone. Even when the last knot came loose and Ponce stepped away, Victorio remained perfectly still. His wide-set, dark eyes were fixed on The Old Apache.

Joto let a little slack into the long lead rope, then sent a ripple running along it. Without any visible preparation, Victorio doubled his legs under him, straightened them and went to his feet in one flowing, catlike move. With his tall, dark legs wide-planted under him, he stood facing The Old Apache, his eyes still fixed unwinkingly on the slight, withered frame.

A low murmur ran through the tense watchers, and no one breathed for a long moment. What held them so still was the massive stallion's complete motionlessness. That, and something else. For the first time, they noticed that those dark eyes were utterly blank, and though no one had told them, each knew that it was not normal, that stillness. They instinctively moved closer together, feeling that sinister something in the air that Ponce had felt moments ago. It grew more intense as the stallion continued to stand there, watching . . . and waiting.

The Old Apache said softly, "No one must come within the

length of this rope, and no one must speak." Then he turned and started toward the corral, some hundred yards away. His movements were slow and calm. Seemingly, he had forgotten what was at the other end of the rope he held He took one step, two, and then he whirled in mid-stride, the whip rising in his hand with a long, sharp whispering sound.

It whispered louder, sharper, then the fang-like lashes darted downward, their tips raking through the thick hide of the stallion's right shoulder and drawing three narrow lines of crimson across the lathered surface. Knowing exactly what would occur the instant he turned his back, The Old Apache had whirled just as the stallion crouched and launched himself forward with deadly intent. Even as Victorio shrieked with pain at the cut of the whip and plunged to a halt, the whip snaked up and back a second time. Victorio reared, flailing the air and shrieking again. The whip curled out, encircled the front legs, and the horse, coming down, could not hold his balance. His legs buckled, and he struck the ground on his side in a choking, blinding cloud of dust.

For a full minute, The Old Apache stood there, watching the animal's futile struggles, then his wrist flipped, loosening the dark coils binding the forelegs. His face was completely blank as he waited for the stallion to rise, and only he saw the dark eyes blaze for an instant with the killing lust. Only for an instant. They closed, and when they flicked open again, they were blank and still. Victorio braced his legs, heaved himself erect and stood motionless.

To Ponce, watching the old man and the stallion, it was clear that Victorio realized his mistake in acting too quickly. It was equally clear that the gray had learned to fear The Old Apache. It was not a nervous, quaking fear; but rather a fear that would make him judge distance and his own timing more carefully the next time. He would not make the same mistake twice. When Joto turned again and started away, Victorio followed at the end of the rope. He walked quietly, never moving his head, never hanging back. And his eyes did not leave the figure of The Old Apache.

With measured strides, Joto paced across the level ground, went under the trees and on through the corral's narrow gateway. Only then did Victorio hesitate. A quiver ran through his frame, and he crouched lower, shuddering with terror. But when the lead rope tightened again, he expelled a long, slow breath that was like a sigh and followed The Old Apache into the corral.

Joto paced on to the center of the enclosure where the stout snubbing post stood. He turned and kept his eyes on the stallion while he took two turns with the rope and tied it. Starting for the gate, he went close to Victorio, and when within ten feet of him, suddenly looked away. The long whip trailed behind him in the dust, like a trained snake.

The gray had followed The Old Apache to within a dozen feet of the snubbing post. As the man went past him, he stood as still as a rock, staring straight before him. His move was too swift for the eye to follow. He went into the air, switched ends and came down, his haunches bunching and propelling him forward like a catapult. He took one reaching stride. His second would put him squarely upon the hateful man-creature who had made the mistake of looking away from him. He was in the air when the rope's slack gave out, and his hurtling, twisting body described a soaring arc which ended in an earth-shaking explosion as it struck the dust. His breath went out of him in a bursting grunt that climbed to a scream of rage and pain as the lash again stung the tender skin of his shoulder.

For a long moment he lay as motionless as death, and for that endless run of time Ponce was certain the thick neck had been broken in the fall. Then, through the drifting dust, he saw the heavy body stir. The head lifted, the legs doubled, and Victorio rose to his feet and stood watching The Old Apache. And again his eyes were utterly blank.

Joto turned and walked to the gate. He waited until Delgadito had secured it with heavy chains, then went to look through the bars at Victorio. His voice, when he spoke after a long time, was a low, soft murmur in the shocked silence that hung over the group.

"He lied," he said, not looking at anyone. "Do you know why, my son?"

Ponce came up and stood beside him, gazing across the open space at the wild stallion. "No, my father," he replied.

The Old Apache did not answer at once. When he did, he still did not look at Ponce, and his voice held a note of regret, almost of sadness. "Because, my son, he is a killer."

The Way of the Stallion

EVERYONE stayed close to the gate until late afternoon. Time and again they crouched to peer through the thick bars at the stallion standing like a dust-mantled statue in the center of the corral. Even now, with the animal behind heavy, high walls, they could not quite believe that the thing had happened. And always their eyes turned toward the dark, shrunken form in the tattered blanket who never once left the gate nor took his eyes from that great creature.

No one spoke of it aloud; but each was aware of the battle of wills going on beween The Old Apache and Victorio. In complete silence and without any movement at all, the two cunning creatures fought with their eyes alone, darting, dodging and trying for one fatal opening in each other's defense. Perhaps it was the strange silence of this which gradually became so strongly felt by the others that they turned, when the light began to fade, and moved toward the steep trail leading to the ledge. They stopped when Joto spoke to them.

"Leave your horses, my friends. Tie them to trees close to this gate, so that Victorio may come to know the scent of horses that belong to man. Juan, when you bring grain for them, bring also one piece of clothing from each person. The time for Victorio to know the taste of new smells is now, while all is strange to him."

Ponce remained with Joto. While the others went from sight and dusk began to gather thickly in the valley, he studied the tall gray. Every bone and muscle in his body ached. When he moved, he had to grit his teeth to keep from moaning; but these things were not the cause of his thoughtful silence.

He was confused, and he could not get his ideas straightened out. He was experiencing the reaction which always follows on the heels of high danger and excitement. Now that the race was run and the prize was within reach of his hands, he grew doubtful, and regret pulled strongly at him. It had started the instant before he had thrown Desert Storm after Victorio and had grown steadily since then. Seeing the proud stallion helplessly penned in by human hands, thrown to the ground and cut by the whispering lash, he felt that a terrible wrong had been committed. Who was he that he should rob Victorio of his freedom? What did he hope to gain? Fame? Desert Storm had brought him that, and he had never wanted it, except for her. Money? He had money enough. And Desert Storm would win more, if it were needed.

He shook his head, trying to dig deeper for the answer that slid out of reach. All he knew finally was that he was no longer sure of himself, nor of what he wanted.

As if reading his young companion's thoughts, Joto spoke. "There is a darkness and a pain in you, is there not, my son?"

Ponce nodded without speaking. He had long since ceased to be surprised at The Old Apache's ability to sense his every thought and mood.

"Even so it was with me one day, my son," Joto said gently "I will tell you."

"When I was young, long, long ago, there was a certain young woman of my people whom I desired for a wife. There was a second young man who wanted her also. Now, among our people there was a custom which will make you tremble, maybe. It was this: When a man wished to take a woman to wife, he asked the woman, and she gave him the 'yes' or the 'no.' But even though it was for her to give the answer, that did not mean that everyone would believe her. If another man desired her, it must be that the two who had asked her must fight, and to the winner the woman would give the 'yes' which everyone would believe.

"When I spoke to this certain young woman, she gave me the 'yes'; but there was another who desired her, and so, according to the custom, I must fight him. Before I did that, I paced the moon and the sun out of the sky three times. I did this because there was in my heart a heaviness and a great doubt. I was not certain that I wanted the young woman, though my heart shouted that I loved her. Still, I hesitated. Still, I doubted. Do you know why, my son?"

Ponce's reply was but a faint murmur in the dusk. "No, my father."

"Because," said The Old Apache, "I was afraid."

Ponce turned, his eyes going to the dark face. In the half-light the features were somehow smoothed out and clearer. The leather-like skin seemed almost without wrinkles, and the eyes were no longer sunken deep in their sockets. For one fleeting moment, he gazed into a face that was again as it had been when youth and strength had flowed through the withered veins.

"Do you hear me, my son?" Joto said more loudly. "I, Joto, tell you that I knew great fear. Though I desired the young woman with every fibre of my being, I told myself that I did not, and I did that because I feared to fight for her!"

The harsh, self-accusing tone changed, and Ponce knew that he had heard words no one else had ever heard. His heart pounded against his ribs with dull, throbbing strokes, and for a moment he could not swallow.

"And did you then not fight, my father?" he asked.

The white head moved from side to side. "I won that fight,

and I took the woman. When I did that, I knew that I had done right to obey the law of the people. Only by risking my life did I become free of doubt. And doubt, alone, my son, can cause fear."

For a long time neither spoke. Ponce's brain reeled with the thing he had just heard. He knew the story had been told him for a purpose, and while he suspected what that purpose was, he hesitated to reach for it.

The silence ran on and on, and it was The Old Apache who again broke it. "Have you no question, my son?" he asked gently.

"Yes, my father," Ponce answered. "Do my doubts come from fear?"

"No," said Joto. "Your fear comes from your doubt. You looked upon Victorio once and desired him so that you risked your life to win him. Now you doubt your ability to break him, and your fear lies in you, so deep that you could not find it."

"But is there no cause to fear him, my father? Will I win?"

Joto nodded. "There is cause. Good cause. As to the winning . . . I will tell you how it must be. You must . . ."

He broke off as low voices came from the foot of the distant trail. "The others return," he said. "They do not want to be away from Victorio. Good! We will wait until they are here. Then I will tell you how it will be, and you will afterwards ask each of them if Joto's words are straight."

Ponce lifted a hand in protest. "I have no need to ask another if your words are straight, my father!" he said swiftly. "I do not doubt your wisdom."

"You believe that . . . now," the ancient warrior growled. "Now it is easy to say you believe. We will see how it is when I have spoken."

Through the gathering darkness the voices came closer. Presently the five white people and three Apaches came in under the trees and drew up around the gate. Barbara stepped close to Ponce.

"Here," she said, thrusting two thick sandwiches into his hands. "I brought you your supper. We all brought our sleeping bags, and we're going to stay here all night. I guess we're as anxious to be near Victorio as you are. He might turn out to be a ghost and disappear, if we . . . *look!*"

Her loud cry turned all eyes toward the center of the corral, and there was a low gasp from the little band of hunters as they stared. The moon was starting its journey across the sky, and in its faint light the gray stallion loomed up like the ghostly being Barbara had mentioned. He was still facing the gate, his head and tail held high, and his massive body stood out sharply against the dark walls of the cliff. There was something unreal and frightening about him.

Joe Marino broke the silence. "Kinda gives you the creeps, doesn't it? The way he stands there without movin' a muscle. I'm glad that rope's on him. And I'm just as glad it's a good stout one!"

Laughter rippled around the tight-pressed half circle, then died as The Old Apache turned and put his back to the gate. "My friends," he said in slow, exact English, "my son for whom Victorio was taken captive would know what lies ahead. I will tell him. Listen you carefully, and if any person among you sees a fault in my words, let him speak."

He waited until the group was seated in a half circle on the warm sand in front of him, then sank down cross-legged. In a deep, musical voice, he began to speak, and the sound of his voice was like the murmuring song of a mountain stream running through a dark cavern.

"The way of the stallion is not the way of other horses. Like a great leader of men, the stallion goes always alone. And always he looks closely at all things that lie along his path before trusting them. He must do this. Always there are those that would strike the leader and bring him down and take his place.

"The way of the stallion is the way of the warrior who must

fight for his rights and for those he loves. In him is a great
hatred for anything that threatens his freedom and his strength
and his mares. In these qualities he is like man; but there the
likeness stops. His own sons he kills, if those sons do not flee
when first he senses in them the danger of the mating challenge. He does this because his sons would kill him, if their
strength were greater than his. It is the law of the stallion.

"We raise horses, all of us. We have stallions, and we trust
them; but there is no man here who would dare turn his
stallion loose on the desert or in the mountains. He would
flee from those he has loved all his life. Maybe he would
return, once . . . maybe twice . . . But if he was not captured
again, he would leave, and the warm memory of his early years
would be buried under the dust of time. He would not come
back, ever.

"You are saying The Iron Duke over there would not run
away. I would have you remember how it went this morning,
when he came face to face with Victorio up there beyond the
lake. He is a kind and gentle stallion, but he would have
thrown Joe Marino to the earth, and if Joe Marino had tried
to hold him, The Iron Duke would have trampled him to
death and gone to his own death at the hoofs and teeth of
Victorio. He would have fought bravely; but he has not the
strength and the cunning of wildness in him, as has Victorio.
He would have died; but if he had not, if he had killed the gray
stallion, he would then have taken the dead one's mares and
kept them, and he would have fought for them to the death.
That is the way of the stallion.

"His way is not the way of the mare. Once only Ponce struck
his Desert Storm in causeless anger, and she was like an inno-
cent girl-child whose father strikes her without cause. For
many days she trembled when she smelled him on the wind;
but she came to know that he had sorrow in him for the deed.
If that had happened again, she would have had a black fear
in her heart forever. This day you saw me twice draw blood

from Victorio with the whip. You did *not* see him leap away in *fear*. There is no shadow of fear in him, and that is why I now tell this young man who is as my own son what must be, if he would make Victorio his own. And know you this, Victorio's way is not the way of other stallions. It is more bad than any I have known. In his mind there is a great black wall behind which he hides. When you look into his eyes, you behold this wall, and you know he is behind it, but you cannot see him. Nor can you make him come out from behind it. He does that only when he believes he can kill you and escape. You saw him come out twice this day, and you saw him leap behind it when he saw that he had failed to kill me. I have seen walls in the eyes of other stallions. Once or twice it was almost as dark and as thick as this one. But always I found a tiny crack, a certain stone, and when the stone was removed, the wall came down. All this day I have probed along the face of the wall behind which Victorio hides. I can find no single stone."

The deep voice stopped, and to Ponce, sitting tense and breathless, it seemed that the wind rushed through the night with greater violence than ever before. Dimly he heard Gil Dreen say, "You've hit the nail on the head right down the line, Joto." And David Forrest added, "I've never heard it put so well." Then The Old Apache was speaking again, and Ponce strained to hear every word.

"I do not know whether Victorio will ever cease to hate all of us whom he has seen and smelled this day. If he could, he would kill us all and grind our bones into the earth, and he would kill every horse here, even the mares, because they have on them the man smell. If he could, he would kill himself at this moment, because there is on him the man smell, and he knows man has made him less than he was before.

"There is in his heart the thing all stallions have, a will that forever seeks to stand against the will of man. It must be broken. Think not that his heart may break. There is no power that could do that. Nor will his spirit be broken, because the spirit is in the heart, and while one still beats, the other lives. The whip may break his will; but never his spirit. Know you that. And until that will lies shattered, the one certain stone will never be seen at the bottom of the wall.

"This we will do.

"We will each day put Victorio into the stall made of logs, and there we will bind him, and there Ponce will touch him. He will never strike the stallion with his hands, for Victorio must never know that the hands of Ponce can cause pain. Always there must be a quietness and a coolness in the hands of Ponce, and often while Victorio stands bound in the stall, Ponce must stand before him and give him the touch of his quiet voice and the steady gaze of his eyes. Never shall the eyes hold doubt or fear or regret. Never must they hold anything but the power of a will that is stronger than the will of Victorio. Know you that.

"After a time, all the bonds holding Victorio in the stall will be taken off, except the hackamore and the one rope. And still Ponce's hands and eyes and voice will go into Victorio, searching through the darkness for the one certain stone.

"On a day, Victorio will come out from behind the wall. Ponce will see him do that, and he will untie the rope holding Victorio in the stall. On that day, Victorio will leave his stall and pretend that he does not know that Ponce is before him. He will pretend that there is in him the desire to be touched by Ponce's hands. Ponce will have the whip, and he will watch the eyes of Victorio, and when he sees the wall go up, he will use the whip. Victorio will fear Ponce. He will fear him all the while he is again put into the stall; but when the hands of Ponce touch him with coolness, he will know that, though Ponce has in him the power to wound, that power is used only when he, Victorio, makes it necessary. And behind his wall he will pace back and forth, thinking about that.

"Days will pass, and often Victorio will come out from

behind his wall, and often he will strike out at Ponce, then leap back to safety when the whip tells him that Ponce knows about the wall and is always waiting. He will do more and more pacing and more and more thinking, and then one day he will wonder what is the sense of hiding, if always he is seen coming out into the open. He will think about that quite awhile. Finally, he will say, 'The wall is no good. I can do nothing when I am behind it, and I can not come out without being seen. I will stop using that no-good wall.' When that happens, Ponce will reach out and with a gentle hand take the certain stone from the wall and throw it away, and the wall will crumble.

"Victorio will not know that this has happened. Every once in a while he will try to jump into that darkness; but it will not be there, and he will be frightened. He will turn to Ponce, asking him for help, and Ponce's hand will touch him, and he will no longer want to hide. After many days, he will want to follow Ponce wherever the young man goes, and when he is alone, he will call for the young man to return. But even then, he will often know anger, and he will often try to kill Ponce. It is the way of the stallion.

"There will come the day when Victorio goes from this valley into the world of man. He will know terror, and when he smells another stallion, he will know again the desire to kill. For a time, it will seem that all is lost; but by this time Ponce will be riding him, and always he will wear sharp spurs and always he will carry a heavy whip. When Victorio moves his muscles a certain way, or turns his head a certain way, or moves his body a certain way, the spurs will dig into his sides, and the whip will tell him it is not wise to let his desire to kill be known to Ponce.

"Soon he will be allowed to run, with Ponce showing him how a good horse runs carrying a man. He will do this as easily as he breathes; but always the spurs and the whip will be with him—and the gentle hands of Ponce, and he will do as he is told, because he will have learned a great respect for Ponce.

"The battle will have ended, and Victorio will forever trust Ponce and respect him and obey him. All this may be."

The voice ceased, and again the night wind roared through the pines. There was a question beating at Ponce's brain; but he dared not voice it in the presence of anyone except The Old Apache. He wished suddenly for the others to take their sleeping bags into the trees so that he might be alone with Joto and ask the question; but The Old Apache was speaking again, and the boy realized that he was answering that unspoken question.

"Whether or not Victorio will ever feel love for Ponce, I do not know. Nor do I know whether Ponce can ever trust Victorio. It is for Victorio to decide. That is the way of the stallion."

10

Near-Fatal Beginning

THE following dawn found everyone up and peering through the gate. There was a hushed nervousness in the air as they saw the big stallion standing exactly where he had been last night. Clearly, he had not moved during the dark hours, for there were no tracks other than those made the previous day. There was something strange and sinister in the way he stood with lifted head, watching the narrow gate, as if waiting for something he knew would come from there.

Gil Dreen's brows were knitted in a deep scowl as he studied the distant animal. "If I wasn't more than half horse myself," he said slowly, "I'd keep my mouth shut. But that stud is no more a cayuse* than The Iron Duke or Desert Storm!"

There was the sound of breaths being sucked in quickly, and everyone turned toward the trainer. David Forrest said, "I suspected the same thing when I saw him in full stride yesterday. Everything about him shouts of hot blood . . . still . . . it's too fantastic to be possible. A man just doesn't let blooded stock go galloping off free as air, if he knows it."

"*If he knows it!*"

* A cayuse (KI-YOOS) is an Indian word applied to an inferior breed of wild horses Contrary to popular belief, cayuses and mustangs are *not* one and the same. The mustang, now extinct, was usually larger than the cayuse, finer-boned, sleeker of coat and swifter.

The words echoed and re-echoed in Ponce's brain. His breathing quickened, and he put out a hand to steady himself against the corral, as the meaning shook him. "But," he said, trying to keep his voice steady, "what if it happened . . . I mean, what if he ran away and no one knew where he went? That could have happened, couldn't it?"

David Forrest laughed and put a hand on the boy's shoulder. "Look, Ponce," he said, his gray eyes twinkling, "you've had one miracle It was impossible for Desert Storm to live, and for her leg to stand up under the punishment it has taken on the tracks. But it happened. That's no less than a miracle, believe me. You're not trying to 'wish' up another, are you?"

Ponce flushed, realizing the truth of the man's reasoning. He dropped his glance to the ground. "No, Mr. Forrest," he murmured. "It was a foolish thought. It could not be."

The man nodded; but immediately his forehead wrinkled thoughtfully. "Still," he said, turning to Gil Dreen, "it's so crazy, it's just possible, after all. If that stud is over four years old and if he isn't a hot-blood, I'll give my stables to the first redhead I meet."

Joe Marino had clambered onto the top log of the gate and had been studying the dark dappled gray. With the eyes of the born horseman, he took in the high, clean lines, the long, curved neck, and the strongly-cut head and wide-set eyes. In the silence following David Forrest's last statement, his voice was unnaturally loud.

"That stud over there," he stated, "is a close relative of Equipoise* or I'm a lion-tamer." He paused, letting his words have their effect on his listeners, then went on in the same definite tone. "I rode Equipoise more times than I can remember, and I know him like I know the Duke . . . maybe

---

* The famous Equipoise (the name means "perfectly balanced") was one of the all-time greats of the track world. A split forefoot prevented him from running in the Kentucky Derby in 1931; but as a four-year-old he raced with phenomenal success, which did not falter until his retirement. Many of his get are today proving his greatness as a sire.

better. If this stud isn't at least a grandson, I'll work free for that redhead Mr. Forrest's going to give his stables to!"

David Forrest had known the Italian rider for several years, and he knew that Joe Marino was not one to make wild statements. Cockey, the slight man might be, at times even boastful; but he had never known him to be mistaken about a horse's breeding or quality. Even so, he was not prepared for this. That any relative of the renowned record-breaker should be found running wild through the high reaches of Arizona's Mogollans was unthinkable. Still . . . Joe Marino knew horses. It was his often-proved boast that he could without hesitation give the color, markings, age and lineage of any horse he had ever ridden. Yes, Joe Marino knew horses. But this idea of his . . .

"That's a pretty strong statement, Joe," Mr. Forrest murmured. "The stud fee on Equipoise was around $5,000, remember? I don't think anyone putting out that much money would be likely to let the results slip through his hands."

Joe Marino was still studying Victorio. "I know what you mean," he said, nodding. "But that stud over there is still a mighty close relative of Old Battlin' Brown!"

Barbara entered the conversation at this point. "Equipoise was a dark brown," she stated. "He wasn't known to throw grays."

The jockey's head bobbed again. "You're right, Barbara; but do you remember . . . ? No, I guess you were too young . . . but there was a tall gray filly that was shipped over from Ireland in '38. Hagar was her name, and she . . ."

David Forrest's voice cut in swiftly. "Let's not talk about Hagar, if you don't mind, Joe."

It was utterly unlike the man to interrupt another in that way, and immediately everyone was looking at him in surprise. They saw his face whiten, and his eyes darken, as if something had suddenly sickened him and angered him at the same time.

Ponce knew something very wrong had happened to the tall

horseman at mention of the filly's name. He had no idea what it was; but when he glanced at Joe Marino, he saw that the jockey knew; because the same look was on his sun-tanned face, and Joe Marino was biting his lower lip, as if to recall the words he had just uttered.

It was The Old Apache who broke the silence. "Think what you want to think," he said mysteriously. "I know what I know, maybe. Now we go to Victorio." He started to climb through the bars; but David Forrest reached out and touched him.

"Wait, Joto," he said in a tense voice. "What do you know? Is it anything about what Joe just said?"

Joto looked slowly around at the man, his eyes dark and blank. Watching him, Ponce suddenly thought of the wall the old man had spoken of last night: Victorio's wall. Now he saw that the aged warrior had one too, and he was behind it now.

"When an Apache does not wish to talk," said Joto, "he says he knows nothing. Now I tell you I know nothing."

He turned and slipped between the bars, leaving the others looking at each other in puzzled surprise. On the other side, he turned again and addressed them all. "When you wish, you shall return to your homes. You have done your work well, and we thank you, my son and I. If, after seven days have come and gone, you wish to return and look upon Victorio again, do that. It will be good for him to learn your smells again."

He stopped, drew a deep breath. When he spoke again, his tone was hard, and he spaced his words very slowly and carefully.

"Speak to no one of what you have done and seen in this place. Do you hear me? *Speak no word of this.*"

He stood, giving each of them his direct attention for a moment, then spoke in his usual guttural tone. "Delgadito, Juan, Dallo Chie, Ponce . . . come you with me."

For a little while the five white people who had been left

at the gate stood looking at each other. Barbara asked suddenly, "Do we have to go right now, Dad?"

"Well," answered her father with a slow grin, "Joto said we *could*, if we wanted to. Personally, I'd like to stick around for the first inning. How about the rest of you?"

There was immediate assent, and everyone crowded up to the gate and stood there watching the five figures moving in on the gray stallion.

It was the tall, soft-spoken Delgadito who went to the snubbing post and untied the lead rope. He moved with the lithe, animal grace of the hunter, his naked upper body glowing like burnished copper in the sun. He knew exactly what to do, and when he started in, he went within arm's reach of Victorio. When he was even with the stallion's shoulder, he suddenly took one long sidestep away.

Like a darting shadow Victorio's left forefoot struck at the Apache, and his head snaked around as he started to strike again. Quick as he was, the whip was quicker. In Joto's hand it writhed up and out, and Victorio went into the air screaming. He came down stiff-legged facing The Old Apache, and it was clear to all that he knew from whence the pain had come, though he did not know how it had happened. For one split second his eyes blazed, then went blank and still. The wall was up, and he was behind it.

Delgadito had not paused in his steady progress toward the snubbing post, had not even glanced around when Victorio struck. He untied the rope, tugged gently and walked toward the bronco stall. Passing to one side of it, he reached the front end, which was closed up with logs. There he lined the rope up, to give a straight pull over the top log of the end, then took a half-turn around a second snubbing post which stood directly in front of the stall. Slowly he began to take in the slack, his eyes quick and narrow on the approaching stallion.

Victorio obeyed the pull of the rope until he was within fifteen feet of the stall's open end. He stopped then, his legs stiffly braced, his head extended on his rigid, curved neck as he dragged the smell of this new danger in through his flared nostrils. All at once he began to shake violently. The mounds of tense muscles along his shoulders and haunches bunched and crawled as if they possessed a life of their own. Sweat sprang out to lay a glistening sheen over the dark gray body and to drip steadily into the thick dust. Like a great crouching cat he squatted there in the sunlight. Then, as the rope grew taut, he went into explosive, terror-driven action.

He reared high, trying to throw himself backwards; but the rope jerked him instantly down, and when he found himself closer to the stall by some three feet, he lunged back, scrambling frantically in the loose dirt. He crouched so low that he was all but sitting down, and his wicked head sawed wildly back and forth, trying to whip slack into the rope that hummed from the strain. He could not get that precious inch of slack. He realized it, and instantly changed tactics. He stood somewhat straighter and jerked back in rapid, evenly-spaced jumps. Still the rope held; still it shortened. With every movement of the stallion, Delgadito took inch after inch of freedom from him, drawing him inexorably toward the open end of the stall.

No one had spoken throughout the brief, bitter struggle. A death-like stillness hung over the corral, so heavy it seemed to hold down the billowing, spurting clouds of dust that rose around the distant stall. But when Victorio found himself almost within the narrow chute, he went stark, raving mad, and his bull-like bellowing and broken shrieks struck through the silence like flaying hands. He went into the air, switching ends with a flipping, rolling motion, and fought to pull straight away. Time after time he gathered himself and lunged, and time after time the rope tightened with a loud, whining sound and snapped him end over end in a ground-shaking fall. His breathing was a harsh cry, and his dappled hide grew red with a thick coating of dust that was turned into mud from the sweat and lather.

Delgadito ceased trying to take up the slack. It was better to let the stallion tire himself out than to force him into the stall. Feeling the thick snubbing post sway and quiver with the strain of the stallion's weight, the young Apache began to wonder if the stall were as capable of withstanding Victorio's struggles as everyone had believed. He took a second turn around the post and stood waiting for Victorio to exhaust himself. From the still expression on his face, no one could tell whether he felt sympathy, disgust, or fear for that rearing, striking mass of fury. Only Joto knew what lay behind that smooth face, and because he knew, he had chosen Delgadito as his chief assistant.

Untouched by the softer emotions known to many of his tribesmen who had lived close to the White Man, Delgadito had the perfect disposition to work with Victorio. He was neither unkind nor cold-blooded; but he possessed the two qualities necessary in a tamer of wild horses—a complete indifference to fear, pain and anger, and that mysterious, animal-like knowledge of wild things. He knew horses better than he knew people. He could perform that often-described-but-seldom-believed feat known as "Talking a horse down."* Without shame, Delgadito had confessed last night that he did not know how to tame Victorio—could not make the stallion hear his voice. Still, his knowledge of horses was such that Joto had immediately decided he was the only one to work with Victorio, except Ponce.

Now the lithe Apache stood calmly waiting for the gray to tire. At the end of a half hour, the driving lunges shortened, the falls came less frequently, and the post ceased to quiver and bend. At last Victorio rose slowly from the dust and stood on

---

* An all-but-lost art today, "Talking a horse down" consists of "the talker" entering the corral and talking to the wild horse. He neither ropes the animal nor touches it; but talks on and on in a calm, understanding tone. It is an established fact that good "talkers" can have the wildest of horses following them about the corral in a matter of minutes. The Navajos are especially gifted in this art. Rarely have white men succeeded as "talkers."

shaking legs, facing the stall. When that happened, Delgadito once again began to exert a steady pull on the rope. When Victorio leaned against it, all but sitting down a second time, Delgadito lifted a hand in a brief signal.

The Old Apache, seeing the signal, spoke to Juan and Dallo Chie, who picked up a long lasso and started around behind the stallion, one on either side. They payed out the lasso between them, and when they were even with Victorio's shoulders, they tightened the rope until its center section touched the crouching stallion's rump. It was as utterly painless as a drifting feather would have been; but at the touch, Victorio leaped five feet into the air, screaming as if a flaming torch had been thrust against him.

When the dust cleared, Victorio was standing less than three feet from the stall. He stood there, snorting and shaking, until the rope again brushed his rump. His second wild leap landed him squarely between the thick logs, and before he could move, Delgadito had taken up the slack and Juan and Dallo Chie had lifted the heavy bar and dropped it into place across the rear of the stall.

It had seemed that the battle was over; but when the stallion found himself prevented from moving either forward or backward, he went mad again. A convulsive strike of his hind legs sent the log bar whirling end over end through the air, to fall twenty feet away, and the stout walls groaned and shook under the impact of the lunging, whipping mass of horseflesh.

Dust boiled thickly around the stall. Calls ran back and forth among the three Apaches, and now and then one of them could be glimpsed, darting in and out of the reddish haze. Then, as suddenly as it had begun, the battle ended. The dust cleared, and Victorio stood sucking air into his nostrils in great draughts. His head was pulled far over the front end of the stall, the heavy bar was again in place behind his rump, and stout ropes were crossed back and forth over his back, to prevent him from rearing. It was impossible for him to move more than a few inches in any direction.

The Old Apache spoke to Ponce. "Now, my son, go you and let your hands cool the fires that rage in him, and let your voice take the darkness from his heart."

He noticed how intently the young man was looking at the distant stallion. With his understanding of others, he knew what was going on inside Ponce's mind, and he said gently, "My son, go now to your friends at the gate. Ask each of them if it be the right thing or the wrong thing we are doing to Victorio." The large, expressive eyes lifted quickly to Ponce, and he smiled one of those rare smiles that seemed to change his whole being. "You would believe me, if you could, my son. I know that, and I have no anger nor pain in my heart, because I know how it is when one must be right beyond all doubt. Go you and ask them."

Ponce's mouth was open. He started to speak, to deny his need for anyone else's word concerning the way Victorio should be handled; but suddenly he whirled and walked swiftly to the gate. "My friends," he said, when he stood before them, "do not think me a child, but I must be very sure that this is not a bad thing we do with Victorio. Tell me, each of you, your thoughts. Mr. Gabe?"

The elderly rancher, like Joto, knew what was troubling his young friend. He said quietly, "Breakin' the wild ones isn't ever a pretty sight, son. But it can't be done just by *wantin'* the horse to be good. Your friends over there are as kind as any I've ever seen."

Ponce looked at Joe Marino. "Joe?"

"I don't know much about wild horses, Ponce," the jockey said honestly. "I know about studs, though, and I know you've got to teach them whose boss in a way they won't forget. You've got yourself a *real* horse, if you do what they tell you."

The young Apache nodded, then swung his glance to David Forrest. "Mr. Forrest?"

The tall horseman did not hesitate. "Every single word Joto said last night about stallions was as straight as a die, son. If you follow his instructions, you'll make a great horse out of that gray—and a happy one."

"Mr. Dreen?"

The stocky trainer cleared his throat noisily. "I go along with Mr. Forrest 100%," he stated. "I don't hold with needless whipping of horses, as you know, and I've never let any of my riders get too fond of one, either; but there have been times I've hauled more than one rambunctious colt to his knees and taught him who was boss. If you want that gray stud to be a horse you can ride, you do just what Joto tells you to. He'll come around."

At last Ponce turned to Barbara. "What are your thoughts, Barbara?"

She swallowed, licked her lips and glanced nervously around, as if feeling suddenly all alone. Suddenly she shook her head, and her words tumbled out in a flood. "I don't know, Ponce! I just don't know! Yes, I do, too! I know they're right, all of them. They know more about horses than I'll ever know—only I know how you feel, too, and I feel the same way—only—"

She paused, out of breath, then nodded violently. "Go on, Ponce!" she cried. "Do what they say. I know it'll be all right. I *know* it will!"

Ponce faced the anxious group a moment longer, nodding slowly, as if admitting something he had known all along but had not accepted. "I thank you," he said, and turned back toward the stall; but Gil Dreen's voice halted him for a moment.

"You do what Joto tells you," the trainer said softly. "And, son . . . I don't think you'll have to use that whip very much."

Ponce's instant smile changed his whole face as he turned and flashed a look of gratitude to the trainer. In all the talk about breaking Victorio, these were the first words that held forth the hope that the punishing part might not be too drawn out. He said in a suddenly-expelled breath, "Thank you, Mr. Dreen!" and ran toward the bronco stall. As he ran, the weight which had settled in the pit of his stomach when he had first glimpsed Victorio bound and helpless the day before began to lift.

He slowed to a walk twenty feet from where the gray stallion stood quivering in the confines of the stall. Slowly he advanced, going along the low wall. He stopped halfway to Victorio's head. For the first time since his capture, he was standing within reach of the animal, and the experience sent waves of chills running up and down his spine.

He had judged Victorio to be somewhat larger than Desert Storm—perhaps even slightly taller and heavier than The Iron Duke; but clearly the stallion stood over seventeen hands. Just as clearly, he weighed not less than 1200 pounds. His hands grew damp as he took in the massiveness of the gray. The thick, cable-like muscles stood out in long, high ridges along the shoulders and spine and hind quarters. Even under the thick coating of clay, they could be seen rigidly set, as if carved from stone. Only the upper third of the body was visible above the logs; but that was enough to show Ponce that Victorio was a giant among horses. Almost, he appeared heavy; but immediately the boy remembered that long, floating action that had kept The Iron Duke and Last Laugh at a safe distance and had demanded Desert Storm's full speed, even after an eight-mile run. No, that massive bone structure and those layers of thick muscles were deceptive. Victorio was not heavy on his feet.

Ponce went closer to the side of the stall, lifting one hand; but The Old Apache's voice stopped him.

"That hand is not cool!" Joto snapped. "It is wet and hot. Get you away!"

Ponce dropped his arm and leaped back, as if stung. He flushed darkly and drew both hands across his thighs, then turned them, palm-up, to the sun. He gritted his teeth, trying to prevent more perspiration from oozing out. Then he relaxed gradually. The palms remained dry, and when he put them to his face, they felt cool. He smiled. The first part of the test was safely past. Now . . .

"Come you here," Joto commanded quietly. When Ponce obeyed, he went on. "Go you to Delgadito and take from him the rope. We will leave you alone with Victorio. He will see you and will draw the smell of you deep into him. You see how the rope pulls his head forward and down? It hurts him and keeps him from moving. He will know it is you who relieve his discomfort, if you move your hands clearly as you loosen the rope ever so little. That will surprise him. It will also please him, and he will start to fight again, thinking he is going to get free. If he does not fight, something is wrong, and you will do well to watch him very, very closely. Talk to him. All the time, talk to him. It makes no difference what words you say. It is only the sound of your voice he will come to understand at first. When he stops fighting, go then and put your hands upon his shoulder. Be you certain the rope is not slack enough for him to be able to reach you with his teeth. If he tries to bite you . . ."

He broke off and slipped the loop of his riding whip off his wrist. It was an ordinary whip, some three feet long and made out of braided rawhide with but a single lash extending from the stock. Joto handed it to Ponce. "Here. If he attempts to bite you, use it. Hit him across the muzzle. That will make him fight some more, so you will wait until he grows quiet before touching him again. Do this now and remember . . . *Do not trust him.* And last . . . *Do not let any slack come into the rope.*"

Slowly Ponce moved around the end of the stall and took the rope from Delgadito. The man stepped back and moved soundlessly away. The next moment, Ponce realized he was completely alone with Victorio. He stood there looking at the head wrenched down toward the base of the snubbing post at that stretched, uncomfortable angle. Clearly the stallion realized the hopelessness of further struggling. Clearly he was defeated. The minutes wore on, and little by little Ponce began to feel pity for the great animal.

With slight surprise, he noticed that Victorio was not paying any attention to him. The large, dark eyes were seemingly glued to the thick snubbing post, a foot from his red-rimmed nostrils.

"Victorio," Ponce murmured in a voice that was like the caress of a gentle hand. "Victorio, will you not look at me? See? My hands are on the rope now, the hands that first touched you, but never harmed you. They will never cause you pain, Victorio."

The stallion's gaze did not waver, the lids did not flicker, and the small pointed ears were flattened against the wicked head. The breath whistling in and out of the nostrils was like the blast from a furnace across Ponce's chest and face.

"Victorio," he said in that caressing voice. "Will you not look at me. Will you . . ."

He broke off suddenly, realizing what the stallion was staring at.

The snubbing post!

With sudden insight, he knew that the post was, in the stallion's mind, a thing of unspeakable horror. He knew also that the limited intelligence of a horse could not possibly have so quickly taught Victorio that a snubbing post was the cause of his helplessness. Yet Victorio knew! His terror rose from his lathered body like a dense fog. And through this fog Ponce groped and found the answer.

Victorio had been snubbed to a post before! He knew what it stood for. And he had suffered because of it. Only that could explain his present attitude, his complete unawareness of Ponce's presence.

On the point of signaling to The Old Apache to tell him of the discovery, Ponce hesitated. After all, he reminded himself, he could be mistaken. If Victorio had feared the post, would

not Delgadito have seen it? That one knew horses like no
other man, so it was said. Still . . . the certainty of being right
was in Ponce, prompting him to loosen the rope and so ease
the stallion's pain. It grew stronger and stronger, and at last it
moved his hand, almost without his knowing, and the rope
slipped. Dimly, the young man realized that he was disobeying
The Old Apache's last warning. But, he was so certain . . .

"Victorio," he said softly, "you have fear of this thing, have
you not? Then, see how I take away the cause of your great
pain?"

He slackened his grip, and the rope slipped farther, giving
the stallion more room. Slowly the thick neck lifted, assuming
its natural curve. When the head was again comfortably set,
the stallion drew in a long, quivering breath, as if not quite
believing the pain was gone. True, the mounds of muscles
along the shoulders and withers did not relax; but that would
come soon, Ponce knew. He knew it beyond all doubt when
the wide-set eyes moved ever so little in their sockets and
looked straight at him. No glint of fire showed in their depths.
They were as liquidly soft and gentle as Desert Storm's.

The answer came to Ponce with shocking suddenness. The
others were terribly wrong about the way to handle Victorio!
They had seen only his bigness and his great strength made
fearsome by terror. They did not know that he wanted affection and understanding: that he would follow the hand of
kindness, but that he would never be driven by the whip. Yet,
all this was plainly seen in that single look the stallion had
turned on him.

With regret for all that had already happened to his great
animal, Ponce responded to the plea in the dark eyes. He said,
"See, Victorio? I touch you, and you feel no . . ."

The next instant he was screaming in terror and agony as
he felt himself lifted from the ground and shaken as a rat is
shaken by a dog. At his first forward movement, the stallion

had darted his head around and fastened his big yellow teeth in the bared shoulder of Ponce.

Wave after wave of white-hot fire streaked through the boy's left shoulder where the teeth were grinding into the hard muscle. He writhed and kicked and lashed out with the whip at Victorio's shoulder; but he was helpless in the grip of those vice-like jaws. Through a swirling fog, he glimpsed the three young Apaches racing toward him, followed by The Old Apache, whose mouth was opening and closing soundlessly. The fog thickened. He felt himself being flung back and forth through the darkness, and he heard his voice going on and on, tearing through his throat in that endless scream. Dimly he saw Delgadito rush in, dimly saw the long lash rising and falling in the young man's hand. And Dallo Chie and Juan were two streaking shadows as they came in and fastened claw-like fingers in the stallion's nostrils and twisted with all their strength to force him to release his hold.

The bood-flecked mouth opened, and Ponce crumpled to the sand under the darting, striking head. He did not lose consciousness entirely. Unable to rise, unable even to crawl away, he lay against the logs, choking on the thick dust struck up by the two struggling Apaches. Through that blinding, reddish haze he saw the men lifted off their feet repeatedly as they clung to the streaming nostrils of the maddened stallion who flung himself back and forth in an attempt to shake them off. And then quick hands grasped his ankles and dragged him to safety.

Even when Juan and Dallo Chie released their holds and darted back, Victorio continued to lunge against the logs of the stall, trying to reach the motionless body ten feet away. He was a raging demon with one thought fixed in his brain. Murder!

The swirling mists cleared for an instant, and Ponce looked up at that striking, darting head in which the eyes blazed like living fires. He closed his eyes, moaning with pain, and rolled over onto his stomach, sickened by the sight. His guilt rushed through him, turning him onto his side. When he looked up, The Old Apache was standing over him, his face gray and drawn, his black eyes holding an accusation.

"My father," said Ponce, gasping as new waves of fire raked through his shoulder. "I forgot about the wall. Even with your words still in my ears, I forgot about the wall . . . and . . . I trusted him."

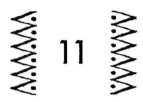

11

The Apache Way

IF THE five white people thought Ponce's injury would keep him out of the corral for any length of time, they were shortly to learn otherwise. During that first hour, while the young man ground his teeth together to keep from crying out with the pain of his torn and bruised left shoulder, they began to think the ancient one slightly less than human. Not understanding the code by which the Desert People lived, they could not understand his attitude toward Ponce.

Never once did Joto speak to the boy, except to order him to lie quietly while he rubbed some evil-smelling salve into the deep wound and bound it with strips of cloth. Plainly his displeasure outweighed any gentler thought or feeling. When the shoulder was securely tied, he turned and walked away through the trees to a spot somewhat removed. Halfway there, he wheeled, saw the three young riders still beside the youth and shouted harshly to them. When they followed him, he motioned for them to be seated, and the four of them squatted cross-legged on the sand. Silence came in under the pines.

This treatment had a calculated effect upon Ponce. He felt no resentment, betrayed no outward pain; but his sensitive feelings were cut to the quick. At first, he wanted nothing so much as to crawl away and die, out of sight of those hard, accusing eyes. This being out of the question, he wanted to explain why he had done as he had. But this, too, was out of the question. The one who must be made to understand was the very one who would not listen.

Hurt and despondent, the young man put his mind to the business of winning back the thing his carelessness had lost. He did not doubt for an instant the ancient warrior's love for him; but he knew that his disregard for Joto's carefully-worded instructions had cost him The Old Apache's respect and trust. And that he must have.

For an hour he lay under the trees outside the corral. A little distance away, his five white friends stood looking at him and conversing in low, puzzled tones. Over there, close to the wall, the Apaches squatted, also talking in low voices. From time to time, Ponce saw one of the young men looking in his direction, and he was quite certain their black eyes held understanding, if not sympathy. Once those voices grew suddenly loud, and he realized with alarm that Joto and Delgadito were quarreling. Clearly he could hear the young horse wrangler shout angrily, then saw him leap to his feet and start toward him. The handsome face was dark and set, and Delgadito did not pause when The Old Apache called loudly, "Come back here, you Delgadito!"

The wrangler came over and squatted down beside Ponce. "How is it, little brother?" he asked in a voice that was so gentle that Ponce could not at first believe it belonged to him. "Is there a thing you would have me do to ease the pain?"

Sick though he was, Ponce still realized what a big thing the stalwart rider was doing in ignoring The Old Apache's command to stay away from him. Among his people, the law lay in the hands of the elders. The young men listened and obeyed, usually without question. To show disrespect for an elder's words was to earn the name of "social outcast," or "rude one." To disobey Joto was nothing less than criminal. It was not done.

Yet, Delgadito was doing it. Fully aware of what his action would cost him in prestige and dignity among his own people, he had come to the injured boy. And his hands that could wield the whip with such deadly skill were cool and gentle as they pushed the tangled hair away from Ponce's mud-caked face.

"Is it in your heart to let the stallion go free, little brother?" he asked in that gentle tone. "Say you the 'yes' and I will do it, whatever The Great Joto may say or do. He is made of stone, that one."

Ponce rolled his head from side to side. "No, big brother," he answered. "He knows it was I who did a wrong thing. I did not remember his words well. I believed that I knew more about Victorio than you, even."

"You have not our years," Delgadito said. "Every man carries with him the memory of a foolish deed. It is better for one to remember what one is told." He paused to reach out a bronze forefinger and gently touch the thick bandage. His eyes held a glint of humor. "It is also less painful sometimes, maybe. But when one sees a brave man lying half dead because of his courage, it is no time for hard looks and cold words. I don't care what The Great Joto says."

Again Ponce rolled his head back and forth. "I will not forget again, big brother. I think that is what The Great Joto knows. Maybe Victorio and I are alike. We must both know pain before we will have wisdom."

Delgadito's narrow black eyes stared down at his young kinsman for a long moment, then his teeth flashed whitely in his dark face, and he reached out and gripped Ponce's right hand tightly. "You are wiser than I," he stated. "I call you 'brother' now, not 'little brother.' So be it." He rose to his full height and faced the distant Apaches. His sudden shout was both loud and angry. "All right, Great Joto!" he yelled. "Your eyes saw the thing as it is, and I was wrong! Will you forever hold your silence over our brother then?"

Joto had been crouched in the shade, glaring at them. With Delgadito's sudden shout, he sprang to his feet, laughing out-right. "Ha!" he shouted back. "You, Delgadito, think you know so much! Maybe you keep your mouth shut next time!"

The lithe rider flushed. "Maybe," he yelled back. "Maybe I will do that! But maybe I will speak what is in my heart, in-stead of hiding it under dark looks, like some old men I know!"

Ponce tried to rise. Alarm was leaping through him again. Would that Delgadito never learn manners? He knew better than to quarrel with a man of The Old Apache's position; yet there he stood, yelling rude things into Joto's very face, almost! Everyone in the country would hear about this, and certainly Delgadito would hear about it for the rest of his life. Everyone would point at him and say, 'There is Delgadito, The rude One, he who called The Great Joto a mean old man to his very face!' If only he would be quiet now, before it was really too late!

"Do not fight with him, Delgadito!" Ponce urged the hand-some rider. "Do not make him angry! It can do no good!"

At the words, Delgadito threw his head back and burst into laughter. "He is not angry!" he said. "I am! I don't like being wrong, and he knows it. That is why he is laughing at me!"

It was true. The Old Apache, coming through the grove, was laughing, though no sound came from his working mouth. He went to Delgadito and slapped the broad, bare back. "Now, wise one," he said, "go you back to the corral and talk your so wise talk to Victorio. We will come soon."

The barely-averted quarrel was over. Ponce drew a great, relieved breath; but instantly he started up again as Delgadito turned wide, disbelieving eyes on him, then glared at Joto. "You are not going to bring Ponce . . ." he began, then clamped his teeth together against further speech and strode furiously away. He motioned for Juan and Dallo Chie to come with him, and a moment later the trio climbed over the gate and disappeared inside the corral.

The Old Apache stood there for a moment, laughing sound-lessly, then turned an amused glance downward. Immediately, all his mirth left him, and his eyes became as cold as ice. "Get up," he commanded.

Without a word, Ponce braced his one sound arm on the sand, rolled and struggled to his feet. He swayed and stag-gered . . . and went to his knees. The pines and ground and nearby corral whirled crazily, blended together and began to fade; but the cold voice cut through his reeling senses.

"I said, *get up*!"

During the past hour, the white people had stood off to one side, held away from Ponce by something they did not under-stand. Without addressing them directly, The Old Apache had clearly indicated to them that they had no part in this. It had happened to an Apache and would be dealt with by Apaches. Sharply, cleanly, he had drawn the line separating his tribesman from his friends for this brief interval. And the friends respected the boundary marker, because they were friends.

But when Ponce was ordered to his feet, only to collapse weakly, Barbara could stand it no longer. She took instant, violent action. She darted through the trees and went to her knees beside the boy and steadied him with her hands. "This is cruel!" she cried, looking squarely up into The Old Apache's cold eyes. "Just plain *cruel*! Can't you see he's too weak to stand? What are you trying to do? *Kill him?*"

The Old Apache's gaze did not waver; but the faintest shadow drifted through the black eyes. Only one experienced in reading the eyes of an Indian could have seen that shadow and known its meaning. Barbara was not that experienced person, and so she could not know that Joto was smiling down at her without moving a muscle of his granite-like face.

He waited until the others had come up and David Forrest had ungently dragged his daughter to her feet and away to a respectful distance. Then his lips moved, letting his dry, guttural voice come out.

"Like all girl-children, this one listens to her heart, instead of to the words of her elders. I speak to her now, so that she will turn her eyes inward and look at this thing calmly.

"This young man . . . this Ponce . . . saw the stallion Victorio and desired to possess him. For this I let him come and call upon you, his friends. For this I called upon three of our people who know the way of horses. For this we have all taken our lives in our hands.

"Ponce is an Apache, and he knows that when one is told a thing, one remembers that thing, or suffers. All of you sat here last night and listened to me; yet none of you listened to me as closely as did Ponce. His breath stopped in his throat while I spoke. That was how he listened. Not an hour ago, I told him each thing he was to do and each thing he must not do. The last thing I said to him was, 'Do *not* let slack come into the rope, and do *not* trust Victorio.' Yet, with these words not yet cold in his ears, he does the two things I commanded him not to do."

He paused, cocking his white head to one side and regarding Barbara out of eyes that were distinctly twinkling. "What happens to you, Barbara Forrest, when you forget the wise words of your father and your mother?"

This was so unexpected that, for a moment, Barbara merely stared. Then she flushed and dropped her gaze. "Well," she answered slowly, "I used to get punished good and proper; but not any more. Now, they cut off my allowance or forbid me to go near the stables or make me do all the housework, or . . ." She broke off, then said loudly, "But they don't make me get up, if I'm too sick and weak to move!"

Joto's lips twitched faintly. "No," he said gently, "they do not. But then . . . they are not Apaches."

"What differences does that make?" Barbara flashed.

"All the difference," Joto replied, still in that quiet tone. "We are all people; but each race and each tribe must hold to its own customs and beliefs, or they will cease to be individuals. The Navajos and The Apaches are Indians; but they are not alike. We do not weave rugs, and they do not know the art of hunting. You make music with your fingers on that thing called the 'piano'; but you cannot make talk with the smoke from fire. You sit in the thing called a 'car' and guide it swiftly across the ground; but you cannot make the hide of a deer as soft as velvet. Each of us does the thing he has learned to do, and that is what makes us what we are.

"Ponce is part White, because he has dwelt among you and learned some of your ways. But he is part Apache still, and I want him to be like the best of his people. If he must suffer to grow, then I will make him suffer. Think you not I have pleasure in this. Each pain he knows, I know also. . . . Maybe it is worse for me, even . . . Because always I have the knowledge that I am the cause of his pain. Yet, when all is said and all is done and I can look upon him as he stands a man, my joy and my pride will be greater than the pain I now know.

"Because Ponce has disobeyed my words, he will rise and go now with me to Victorio. He will do that because he knows in his heart the wrong he has done. The taming of Victorio cannot stop, cannot wait. If Ponce falls to the ground, then will I drag him to the stall, and there will I let him lie, because Victorio must come to know the smell of him through all the days and nights to come.

"If you cannot believe my words, if you cannot bear to look upon his suffering, then go you away, Barbara. It may be that you could not believe me, even if you would. If that be so, I have sorrow for it. You have in you a beauty and a gentleness. When you add strength and wisdom to those, you will be a woman . . . a good woman."

He was silent, looking deep into Barbara's eyes. What he

read in the brown depths pleased him, and he grunted low in his throat and nodded. Then he moved over and bent to place a hand under Ponce's right arm. He said gently, "My son, stand beside me now." And when Ponce slowly rose, he turned and led the boy toward the corral.

12

While Time Stood Still

ALL that afternoon, The Old Apache seemed preoccupied. Time and again he sank down cross-legged on the sand and buried his chin on his chest, as if about to doze off, only to rise and pace back and forth. From time to time his lips moved silently, his head shook impatiently, and his hands struck each other, as if in anger. He spoke to no one, looked at no one. He shut them all away from him as effectively as if he had entered a room and closed the door behind him.

When Barbara and Gabe had the supper laid out on the blanket that served as a table under the trees, the girl went to find him. Some distance back in the grove, she ran across the prints of his moccasins in the sand and followed them at a trot. She skidded to a halt suddenly, as Joto appeared, seemingly out of nowhere, and held up a hand in a warning gesture. She opened her lips; but closed them on silence as the thin hand waggled commandingly. Puzzled, she stood there looking at him; but when the hand motioned her back whence she had come, she turned and ran.

Reaching the fire, she related her experience, finishing with: "So I suppose we'd just as well go ahead and eat without him."

Delgadito looked up from the bridle he was repairing. "He is listening for something," he stated quietly.

"What?"

"I know not. He will tell us when and if he sees fit to do so, perhaps."

They ate. Afterwards they sat around the fire talking, mostly about Victorio and his murderous attack upon Ponce, and about the seemingly impossible task of breaking the mountain stallion. When the fire was a bed of coals, they retired to their sleeping bags and blankets. And still The Old Apache had not returned from his wanderings and meditations.

Beneath a tree, Ponce moved uneasily in his blankets, trying without success to find a favorable position for his injured shoulder. At last he dropped into fitful slumber, but awoke from time to time and lay staring up through the interlaced branches at the fleecy clouds scudding before the night wind. Once he thought he heard voices somewhere far back in the trees; but when he raised himself slightly and turned his head that way, he could hear nothing but the wind crying through the jagged escarpment rimming the valley.

He slept again, and when he awakened, it was from the touch of a hand on his shoulder and a voice saying, "Follow me, my son." He was instantly on his feet, as alert as if he had not slept at all.

A few yards away, he glimpsed The Old Apache, bending over his tribesmen. He heard no sound, but the three young men promptly rolled from their blankets and followed Joto— and Ponce went with them. On noiseless feet they stepped around the forms of the sleeping white people, heading for the corral.

"He has heard something or seen something or learned something . . ." Ponce thought, "something important. He moves with the strength and the swiftness of youth. Suddenly he has become someone I have never seen before."

At the corral gate, The Old Apache halted and waited for the others to come up. When he spoke, his voice was startlingly loud, his words quickly uttered.

"Listen you well. I must not waste words, for the thing is upon me, and I know not how long it will stay. All this day I have tried to remember a thing. Just now it came to me." He paused, looked at each of them in turn, then announced in a harsh whisper, "*I have the voice!*"

As one man, the three Apache riders sucked in their breath and tensed, their eyes becoming riveted to the ancient warrior.

"You?" Dallo Chie whispered in awe. "You, my father, are one of *those?*"

"Once," Joto replied, nodding quickly. "Maybe twice . . . It was a long time ago . . . long, long ago . . . I was a mere youth and knew not that I had the voice . . . until it came suddenly to me."

Ponce looked from one to the other, understanding nothing they were saying. "This voice . . ." he began, but The Old Apache cut him off with a movement of his hand.

"Delgadito will tell you," he said. "Straps I need, and the whip and blanket and saddle. Dallo Chie, go you with Juan and bring them to me in the corral. Go you quickly . . . and . . ." He paused, stood in thought for a moment, then went on. "Say nothing to the white ones. They would not believe, and there is no time for talk. Go you now!"

He bent, slipped through the gate and went rapidly toward the bronco stall. Delgadito turned to Ponce, and the boy saw tension and excitement grip his handsome, dark features.

"You know nothing of the voice?" he asked. When Ponce shook his head, he began to speak quickly. "It is a rare gift. More Navajos have it than Apaches; but a few of us have been known to possess it. I did not know that The Great Joto was one of those chosen few until this moment. They call it 'The Voice,' do the horse-tamers. It is a tongue wholly unlike any other. The words make no sense to other men, but they have a power over horses, a terrible power which none can resist. Once it touches a horse, he is not ever again the same."

"But," Ponce broke in, "you cannot mean that mere unknown words succeed where all the arts of great horse-tamers fail! I cannot . . ."

"Call you The Great Joto a fool?" the slender rider demanded harshly.

Ponce was stunned by the sudden-flaring anger in the usually calm man. "Never that! It is only . . ."

"The voice he has within him this night, I tell you! Have you grown so far from us that you dare to look upon our ways with the doubts of a white man? I had not thought so. I do not like that in you, my brother! But however weak your knowledge of our ways, you will see a thing this night which may restore your faith in those things our forefathers knew well!"

He broke off speaking as Dallo Chie and Juan came from the shadows of the trees, carrying the gear which The Old Apache had ordered. Juan said, "Come silently," and slipped into the corral. A moment later, they were all standing halfway between the gate and the bronco chute. Dallo Chie lifted both hands, signaling them to remain motionless where they were. They fixed their attention on what was going on over there where Victorio stood helpless between the log walls.

In the bright moonlight, The Old Apache's hair was an aura of silver, his naked upper body tinged with an unreal bluish light. He was standing motionless in front of the giant gray, and the unceasing murmur of his voice ran through the moonlight like a shimmering thread. He spoke rapidly, clearly and without any inflection in his tone. The language was one Ponce had never before heard, seemingly comprised mainly of a series of low moans, long hissing consonants, and throaty murmurings.

Ponce could not have told how long he stood there with that mystic voice weaving its spell around him in the night; but when at last he saw Joto move in closer to the stall, he shifted his weight. The slight action sent pains knifing up his legs, and he realized with surprise that they had gone to sleep. Glancing up, he noted the position of the moon. It was directly overhead, so that no shadows slanted across the hoof-torn sand of the corral. His breath stopped in his throat suddenly, and he made an involuntary movement which Delgadito halted with a quick gesture of his hand.

The Old Apache had walked forward and laid one hand on Victorio's rigid neck.

The stallion remained half-crouched in the stall from the moment Joto stopped in front of him. While the voice worked at him, he stared straight into The Old Apache's face, his eyes set and blank. When the hand touched him, he sank still lower, and an awful trembling wracked his iron-muscled frame. Nor did it pass quickly. For long minutes he shook violently, as if in great agony, and each breath he sucked in through his distended nostrils was a shuddering, protesting moan.

Still the voice filled the night. Still it curled around the flattened ears, pierced the dense protective hair within them, writhed inward until the murderous animal was crazed with fear. It would not cease, would not slow, would not give him time to gather his dazed senses for resistance. It was merciless, yet kind, inexorable, yet gentle, and it was a thing Victorio could not rend nor maim nor banish. Sweat broke out on his neck and flanks, turned to lather and spread up along his sides, to drip onto the sand all around him. And gradually the terrible tremors lessened.

"Oh! Uh! Oh! Aeeeeieiiiiahohah stal soieee!"

The words that were not words, but sounds run together, dropped to a lower key, and again Ponce was impelled to move as The Old Apache worked his way along Victorio's foam-covered side. He felt Delgadito's warning hand on his arm and forced himself to stay where he was. Gradually the realization of what he was witnessing overcame his fear for Joto. From the shadows of his long-forgotten youth, Joto had plucked a memory and shaped it into a powerful weapon which he was using to accomplish what they had all failed to accomplish so far.

With matchless patience, The Old Apache worked along one side of the stallion, then up along the other until he was once again beside the wicked-looking head. The head swung about, and in the eyes of the stallion lay a great question. They gazed at the gnarled figure whose hands and voice were at once the most terrible and the most kind things he had ever known. They followed that figure as it moved to the snubbing post and untied the rope. And when Joto went to the rear of the stall and commenced to remove the logs there, Victorio turned his head so that he would not lose sight of him. The ears which he had always kept flattened in the presence of the hated man-creature were pricked sharply forward, flicking and twisting constantly to catch the smallest sound coming from this strange creature of the night.

The Old Apache tugged lightly on the rope and Victorio, sensing freedom, lunged backward out of the chute and whirled to bolt. The voice cut across his dazed brain, pivoting him in his tracks, and, with a loud snort, he commenced circling, moving with long, effortless bounds. Once he veered in sharply; but the voice struck him with an almost physical force, and he shied away. Without being aware of it, he was being worked into an ever-lessening circle as the rope was shortened inch by inch.

He was going so close to The Old Apache now that he could not balance himself for the gallop and so dropped to a trot. The rope shortened still more, and he was walking around less than five feet from Joto, whose voice never paused nor wavered; but went on and on, like the unceasing night winds of the mountains.

"*Ho! Aieeeiii ho!*" The Old Apache said quietly and took the last yard of rope into his hands. "*Ho! Uh kolah!*" he said and ran his free hand along the wet neck and shoulder of the stallion and on down to the slender foreleg. For a long time he stroked that leg, then picked up the foot as a blacksmith would have done. Without changing his tone, he spoke to Juan, who had gradually moved nearer. "Come now, you. Bring me the straps and the whip."

Juan moved in, handed him two straps with buckles and the long whip.

Joto took the things, still talking to Victorio, still holding the foot. Then, too swiftly for the eye to follow, he slipped one of the straps around the leg, just below the fetlock, and drew it tight. He passed the end around Victorio's forearm and buckled it. Supporting the bound leg on his thigh, he slipped the other strap over the stallion's back and buckled it also. Next he fastened the strap that bound the leg to the improvised surcingle.

Victorio was half-rearing now, staggering slightly. As a realization of his helplessness struck him, he went up on his hind legs and flailed the air with his free forefoot. The Old Apache gave a final hard yank to the straps and leaped to safety.

Victorio promptly went mad. Hobbled and off balance, he lunged at Joto, and the old Indian danced farther back. He flipped his hand that held the whip, and the cracker snapped sharply; but the lash barely grazed the bulging shoulder.

Ponce turned away. "I cannot watch!" he whispered. "I cannot . . ."

Delgadito said, "Stand you! The Great Joto knows what he is doing. Would you refuse to witness this thing which you will never see again?"

When Ponce turned back, Victorio was no longer staggering and lunging about. He was down on the sand and The Old Apache was crouched over him, rubbing his head, stroking the foam from his neck, and whispering into his ear.

And the mountain stallion was lying quietly under the hands and the voice, as if listening to what Joto was saying. Almost, it seemed to Ponce, he understood the strange words.

Joto spoke to Dallo Chie. "Bring those things which he must wear."

Dallo Chie took the saddle and blanket over and laid them near the stallion. Joto dragged them closer and let Victorio smell them for several minutes. Next he proceeded to rub them back and forth over the prone animal, slowly, deliberately, pausing often to address the lathered gray in a questioning tone. When even the detested oil-coated things failed to rouse Victorio from his lethargy, Joto lay down full length across the sweaty body and moved his arms and legs all over him. And still Victorio did not resist.

"Ha!" Joto exclaimed, beckoning the others over. "Ha!" he said again, sliding to the sand and straightening. He walked all around Victorio, pausing every foot or so to prod the animal with a mocassined toe. Seeing complete victory, he moved up and sat on him and addressed him in Apache. "Big horse, great horse, horse who was wicked and filled with the killing lust, I have given you words that have destroyed the evil thing in you and gentled you. You will remember them always. From this night onward, you will be subject to man. Know you that!"

Standing beside the motionless stallion, Ponce realized fully for the first time the tremendous task which The Old Apache had performed. Not yet could he wholly believe that Victorio was gentled. It had all happened in so short a time. Then he glanced up and noted that the moon was gone. He looked all around and saw each pole of the corral clearly outlined by the rays of the rising sun. The night was gone! The Old Apache had worked with Victorio for some six hours without pause. Glancing at his ancient friend, he saw the deep marks of fatigue and strain lining the parchment-like face and realized how much Joto had given of himself this night.

He bent to touch the stallion's shoulder, but Joto said, "Not yet is he like your Desert Storm, my son. Take care lest your hand tell him you still doubt him."

Suddenly, with the words, Ponce had doubts no longer. He went to one knee and laid both hands firmly on the wet hide in which the black dapples showed like large circles of ink drawn upon absorbent paper. There was no hesitation in his hands. He said in a shamed voice, "I did have doubts, my father. I could not believe . . ."

"Ha! I doubted myself!" Joto said and chuckled drily. "For one moment, before I started, I looked into his eyes and saw the great pride and hatred burning in their depths, and I doubted. But it is done."

"I have no words . . ." Ponce began.

The ancient warrior made a brushing motion with one hand. "Words! Words! They are made of air and turn into air, once released from the mouth. You did not know it, but your heart knew this thing would happen, my son, else you would have torn yourself from Delgadito's hands and run to save me from your big gray demon. Your heart knew."

"Will you saddle him now?"

"No. For the first time he has suffered enough. Almost the devil in him killed him before it would die. See how the water still streams from him? The fires have not yet wholly died out. To excite him now would be to kill him, my son. Tomorrow, perhaps, when he has had time to think of all that has happened, he will carry the saddle with you in it." He looked away, then gave Ponce a sidelong glance. Only another Indian could have caught the shadow of a twinkle in the black eyes. "You are surprised? But why should you? You wanted this old pile of bones so badly you were willing to risk all our necks to get him. Now will you sit in the shade and cover your eyes and have *me* fall apart trying to break him?"

"Break him?" Ponce exclaimed. "But he is now . . ."

"Quiet? Even so, but think not he will stay this way forever. I have but taken the killing urge from him, not the pride that will make him fight to remain a free horse. He will battle you mightily, my son, but in the end, perhaps, he will say, 'enough!' Think not I have torn the wall down. I have but loosened one small stone so that it cracked ever so little. Your work is still before you. Know you that."

"Oh," Ponce said, and flushed as the others burst out laughing.

And that was the way Barbara found them when, after waking and finding them gone, she came to the corral gate to summon them to breakfast. For one long moment she stared, open mouthed, at The Old Apache calmly sitting on Victorio's neck, at Ponce just as calmly stroking the lathered shoulder and at the three young men standing nearby laughing. Then her ear-splitting yell sounded in the bright morning sunlight, summoning the others.

13

Ponce Makes Up His Mind

FOR two days silence reigned in the corner of the valley
where the corral stood. Victorio no longer shrieked his fury to
the cloudless heavens when Ponce's hands touched him. Nor
did he attempt to break the bonds holding him in the stall.
Though he crouched, quivering, each time the boy's hands ran
over him, there was a gradual lessening of his terror, or so it
seemed to the young Apache. It was Delgadito who corrected
that impression, and his words made Ponce's blood run cold.

They were standing in front of Victorio's outstretched head
as the stallion stood in the stall on the third morning. No
muscle moved along the high, deep shoulders. The wide-set
eyes were unclouded, practically docile. One could almost
believe the stallion had decided against doing further battle.

"He is so quiet, so gentle looking, is he not?" said the
muscular rider. "One looks at him and thinks, 'But surely his
hunger and thirst and the discipline have made a different
horse of him. No?"

"One could believe that," Ponce agreed.

"And then," Delgadito went on, "one looks very closely and
sees something far, far beneath the soft eyes. Do you know
what the mountain stallion thinks then, brother?"

"No, brother. Tell me."

"He thinks *murder*. One sees it as a faint, faint shadow far behind those eyes, and one says, 'Now this horse has decided that waiting is better than fighting. I will be a fool if ever I forget that. I will be more than that. I will be a *dead* fool.' "

Ponce started, then turned and searched for the shadow Delgadito had mentioned. At first he saw only the tiredness that was pulling the stallion down, hour after hour, and the defeat and resignation. Then, so faint as to be only the suggestion of a shadow, he found it. And again he shivered, as if a cold wind had passed over him. He said quietly, "Delgadito, what is to be done? Will nothing show him that we would not cause him pain willingly?"

Delgadito's voice took on a tense, hard note. "Let not your heart be softened with pity for this devil, brother. Never forget he knows all too well that he fooled you three suns ago. He is waiting for another chance. He has given up hope of freedom. Now he waits only to kill. I have known others like him, though none so bad. Two of them I won with 'The Talking'; but this one does not hear me. Watch."

He reached out and took hold of the rope, and Ponce saw the stallion's eyes change ever so little, darkening and going motionless at the touch. Then Delgadito began speaking in a low, sing-song tone that was unlike anything Ponce had ever heard. The Apache words were slurred and indistinct; only the rhythm remained constant, rising and falling like deep water passing over unseen stones. There was a kind of hypnotic cadence to the voice. Vaguely Ponce knew that his own upper body was swaying gently in time to the rising and falling tone. The effect was powerful, mysterious, but it did not touch the stallion. He remained perfectly still, slightly crouched, his eyes never changing, never moving. When the voice ceased, there was no indication from the flattened ears that they had ever received it.

"You see that?" Delgadito asked, half angrily. "Always before it has had its power; but not with this one. Do not forget that!"

"What, then, can be done?" Ponce cried wildly. "Have you no answer?"

"Wait!" said the handsome wrangler. "That is the answer."

At this point, Joto slipped through the bars of the gate and approached. He stopped close to the stall and regarded the motionless stallion for a long time. "Seven suns have come and gone," he said slowly, "and each shows more flesh fallen away and the bones sticking out farther. He did not touch the oats nor the fresh grass nor the water you left for him."

Ponce shook his head. "Will it go on until he lies dead, my father?"

Again Joto was silent for a long time. At last he shook his head. "No, it will not. He is too proud to die, I think." He took a squat earthen jar from under his blanket and held it out to Ponce. "Here. Take you some of the medicine on your fingers and rub it into the cuts. It will ease his pain."

Ponce's nostrils dilated as he removed the lid and caught a whiff of the dark, jelly-like substance in the jar. He knew the marvelous healing powers of the salve from past experience, for it was the same medicine which had been rubbed into Desert Storm's fractured foreleg a year ago. He found a toehold between the second and third log and lifted himself until he could reach Victorio's shoulders, where long gashes had cut through the gray hide. Taking a little of the ointment on the ends of his fingers, he began to massage it into the wounds.

At the first touch, Victorio crouched lower, a deep tremor running through him. Other than that, he made no move throughout the doctoring process; but neither did he change his crouching stance. Only when Ponce finished and stepped away did he resume his normal standing position. But as the powerful mixture began to work and draw the soreness and the fever from the cuts, there was the faintest sign of lessening tension in the big body. Seeing that, the three Apaches exchanged knowing glances, and Ponce felt hope once again begin to throb inside his chest.

They day wore on. Never was the stallion left alone. Hour after hour, one or more of the Apaches were with him. Sometimes they talked to him in low, unhurried voices. Sometimes they sang one of their long, monotonous chants. And sometimes they walked around and around the stall. But they would not leave him.

Through the hottest hours of mid-afternoon, The Old Apache dozed in the sun against the rock wall, his white head sunk on his chest. As the shadows began to lengthen, he roused, got to his feet and returned to the stall where Ponce and Dallo Chie were pacing back and forth within sight of the stallion's eyes.

"Dallo Chie," he ordered, "go you and tell Delgadito and Juan to move everything into the corral. We live here now."

As the man strode away to carry out the order, Joto explained, "Victorio thinks we will go away some time and leave him alone. He thinks he is boss, maybe. We will show him how wrong he is. He will see us every time he opens his eyes and he will smell us every time he draws a breath and he will know then that he is never going to be alone again."

"But," Ponce asked, "will he not refuse to eat so long as we are near?"

"He does that anyway. When his belly begins to jump and curl with the pain of hunger burning in it, he will eat; not until then. But I think that is happening already. I think maybe tonight he will steal some of that grass over there—and some of that water and those oats. He will do that, I think, when we are asleep."

The three young men came into the corral, loaded down with blankets, cooking utensils and foodstuff. The camp was set up against the wall, directly in front of the stall, and while supper was cooked and eaten, Victorio was obliged to look on. Time after time he turned his head, staring away from his captors, but gradually it dawned on him that they were there to stay, and he ceased pretending to ignore them. After that, he kept his unwinking gaze fastened on them.

As dusk piled up thickly along the high walls, Delgadito and Ponce approached the stall. The man lifted the rear bar from its place, and Ponce untied the rope from the snubbing post. Like a racer breaking from the starting gate in reverse, Victorio shot out of the stall and streaked to the far side of the corral. Twenty feet from the gate, he rose in a soaring leap. The impact of his heavy body crashing into the chained barrier set the walls of the corral weaving and groaning in protest, and for a moment the stallion was hidden in the thick cloud of dust struck up by his fall. He reappeared almost instantly, flashing along the high walls. He came on around, then veered sharply away from the stall. He lost his footing in the sand, turned end over end and skidded a dozen feet. He leaped up and lunged away, still at a dead run.

A dozen times he circled the corral, his speed gradually lessening. He dropped from a laboring gallop to a long trot, then to a walk. Finally he stopped altogether, his long, dark legs trembling with exhaustion. Plainly, he was a sick horse. His refusal to eat or drink had dragged the flesh off him until he was a mere skeleton of his former self. His breath rasped in and out of his open mouth as he fought for air. Short days ago, he would not have been even slightly winded after a run such as he had just made. Now he was on the verge of collapse. When he could breathe less painfully, he walked unsteadily to the gate, there to stand looking into the night-curtained distance from whence the scent of his mares drifted to him on the cool wind.

In the darkness, The Old Apache's voice held a note of sadness as he said, "Once we Apaches were like him. We drank freedom on the wind and we ate strength in raw meat. We knew no master. We feared no thing under the sun. All people feared us. Then the White Man came. The land was taken from us. Then we drank hatred in the wind and choked on defeat in the dust. And for a time there was starvation stalking our camps and death in our hearts, and we longed for the freedom that was forever gone. The wise ones said, 'Better to eat the food our hated captors throw to us than to die. Better to live with pride than to die with shame.' And so it was done."

He paused, then finished in a voice that was little more than a whisper, "I know how Victorio feels. I know "

"Even so it was," Delgadito muttered. And Juan and Dallo Chie echoed the words in the darkness. "Even so it was."

Ponce swallowed with difficulty. After a time, he managed to find his voice. "And what of now, my father? Would you have things as they once were?"

The Old Apache uttered a short, dry laugh. "Dreams are for the sleeper, my son. I have no worries and no hunger. I can dream my dreams in the suns of my last days. It is enough."

No one said anything more for a long time. Finally Juan rose to unroll his blankets. "That stud had better stay on his own side of this place," he grumbled as he dug a place in the sand for his shoulders and hips. "I don't want him stomping around on top of me. I don't like this much."

Dallo Chie's laugh exploded. "Big, brave man you are!" he exclaimed sarcastically. "Maybe you better sleep in the bronco stall! Victorio won't get you there!"

The three men laughed at the idea of the stocky rider hiding inside the stall. While Juan went on grumbling to himself, they unrolled their blankets and prepared for sleep.

"He will not come near this place," Delgadito said, grunting and stretching. "He would try to climb over the wall rather than come within rifle shot of us. Only when the rope tightens does he want to kill."

Ponce lay down on one of his thin blankets, drew the other one over him and tried to sleep, but for a long time his thoughts worried through him, holding him awake. Gradually, however, fatigue took its toll, and he drifted into dreamless sleep. Once during the night he roused, awakened by faint sounds that seemed to come from the far side of the corral. He raised himself to his elbows, wincing as sharp pains shot through his left shoulder. He lay there listening, but the sounds did not come again, and at last he lay back.

Ponce awakened in the first flush of dawn to find Delgadito's blankets empty. Looking around, he spied the tall man coming toward him from the gate. He jumped up, as the other motioned to him, and ran through the chill gloom, wondering what had happened to bring that wide smile to his friend's handsome face. A moment later, he was standing in front of the gate, looking down into two empty metal buckets. Last night one had been full of water, while the other had held a measure of oats. A pile of green grass had lain between them. Now buckets and ground were bare.

Victorio had lost the fight with his stomach!

Ponce leaped into the air. "I will put more water and oats and grass here!" he shouted. "Now Victorio will know it is better to eat and drink than to fight himself and us! He will not die!"

Delgadito's eyes glinted with amusement, but he reached out and held Ponce still. "No," he said, "he will not eat while we can see him—not for a long time. Anyway, it will be better to let his hunger torment him a while longer, so he will appreciate more the food and water you give him. You must make him admit it is you who are keeping him alive."

Ponce nodded, seeing the logic in the other's words. With Delgadito, he returned to the camp site, where Juan and Dallo Chie were setting about preparing breakfast.

"So," The Old Apache called out to them, "the fast is over, is it? So much has been won then."

"Yes, my father," Ponce answered with a wide smile, "he will not die, after all."

Juan looked up from the bacon he was turning over the coals. "He never wanted to die," he stated bluntly. "All the time he went hungry just to worry us. He is no good, that stud of yours!"

As usual, Dallo Chie could not resist the temptation to poke fun at his grumbling kinsman. "You don't like him because he has the pride you lack!" He laughed. "If you were in his place, you would eat first all the food you could grab, then think about fighting and hating your enemies!"

On the point of hurling a loud denial at his friend, Juan closed his mouth and bit his tongue to keep from laughing with the others. He returned his attention to the bacon, making low noises in his throat. No matter how hard he tried, he could never make anyone believe he was as ill-tempered as he pretended.

The sun was just lifting over the eastern wall of the valley as Ponce and Delgadito walked through the dust toward Victorio. They moved slowly, making no unnecessary motions with their hands, and they stopped fifty feet from the stallion, to give Juan and Dallo Chie time to come in from either side. When all four were in place, they moved slowly forward, closing up the half-circle. To escape, Victorio would have to dash between two of them, and that he would not do. His eyes were fixed on the long whip Delgadito carried. He stood perfectly still as Ponce stepped ahead of the others and picked up the trailing lead rope.

With Delgadito walking slightly out to one side, Ponce turned and led the stallion to the stall. There he passed the rope over the end logs, made a half turn around the snubbing post and took up the slack as Victorio came up. For one moment it seemed that the usual battle would not take place this morning. While everyone stood waiting in tense silence, the stallion walked to within three feet of the narrow structure. He appeared calm, almost willing to do what he knew was expected of him. But, with one forefoot off the ground, he exploded into furious action.

He whirled and threw his weight against the rope, but, instead of turning a sommersault and landing on his back when the rope tightened, he let himself go limp. The force of his lunge swung him around, and he snapped out straight at the end of the rope, like the end person in the game of crack-the-whip. The snubbing post creaked and bent. The rope hummed like a taut bowstring. But both held.

Failing in his first shrewd maneuver, Victorio squatted on his haunches and flung himself from side to side, his head whipping crazily. He grunted with every lunge, and short, choking breaths gushed from his wide nostrils and gaping mouth. Dust rose thickly around him as his back-clawing hoofs tore up the earth.

Suddenly, Delgadito did something he had never done before. He sent the whip curling up and out, but instead of touching Victorio with the lash, he snapped his wrist back a split second sooner than usual. The three rolled lengths of rawhide popped together with the loudness of a pistol-shot, short inches above Victorio's flattened ears.

The stallion made no pretense of being deaf to that nerve-shattering noise. He leaped into the air as if stung. His jump put him into the stall, and before he could collect his scattered senses and set about his usual struggle, he found his head yanked forward and down by the rope.

"So," Joto stated triumphantly, "he now knows the sound of the whip! He finds it is better to jump before the lash touches him. Good!"

Ponce was talking to the terrified animal in Apache, as he had done constantly throughout the preceding three days. With his hand on the rope, less than three inches away from the distended nostrils, he crouched and looked straight into the flat black eyes, trying to reach behind the darkness there.

After an hour, Joto came over and stood watching and listening.

"Let his head come up," he ordered quietly. "Let it come up and take my whip and keep talking to him. When you feel the time is right, put your hand on his neck. And—" he paused, an amused glint in his eyes, "remember your shoulder, my son."

"*As if I could forget it!*" Ponce thought. Each time he moved his upper body, hot pains flashed through the bruised muscles and torn ligaments. Though it was bound tightly, the wound still hurt. He would carry the imprint of Victorio's large yellow teeth all his life. No, he would not be likely to forget it. He looped the quirt over his right wrist, continuing to speak in a quiet, even tone.

Without knowing how it had happened, he suddenly discovered that he was a changed person. One moment he was a boy whose feelings were all too close to pity for the captive giant in front of him. The next, he was a young man with but one thought in his head: to conquer this seemingly insane creature who would not acknowledge the fact that he, Ponce, was on the earth, even! He was not angry, but he was more determined than he had ever been in his life.

"Victorio," he said levelly, "you have not known me very long, but it does not take you very long to learn a thing. Now hear me. I am tired of *asking* you to look at me and to listen to me. Now I am *telling* you! I am going to let you lift your head, and then I am going to put my hand on your neck. You can try to sink your teeth into me again, if you wish, but if you do, you are going to have a sore nose. Know you that. You think you are a big, bad horse. I think so, too. But before long you are going to be a big, *good* horse. You had better believe that."

He did not realize that he had raised his voice, until he heard Delgadito say in a pleased tone to Joto, "Now we can breathe again, my father. Our brother has come to his senses."

He did not turn. All his attention was on the stallion and the
rope he was beginning to loosen. Slowly, steadily, he let it
slip, until the chiseled head regained its high set on the arching
neck. Then he moved closer, sliding his feet through the
sand in short steps. He could feel the heat rising from the
stallion's wet shoulder and neck as he lifted his injured left
arm and laid his palm flat against the dappled gray hide.

A tremor ran through the thick muscles of that neck. It
moved away, bending, and Ponce whirled like a panther and
brought the riding whip down across the darting, reaching
muzzle. He was talking all the while. He went right on talking
as Victorio's scream knifed through the morning air. And his
left hand continued to stroke the heavy neck, as if the enraged
mountain stallion were the most docile of pets. Three more
times the head darted around, aiming for the young man's
shoulder, and three more times it was flung high as the quirt
stung the tender muzzle. But the quiet, level tone of Ponce's
voice never faltered, never varied.

It was Delgadito who saw the stallion's eyes change. It happened so quickly, was gone so quickly, that for some time he could not be certain he had read the expression correctly. He said nothing, but his head began to move up and down as the suspicion grew to a certainty. His eyes had not played a trick on him. Victorio was surprised and Victorio was puzzled. He might hate this boy who insisted on stroking his neck, but he had begun to respect him. Of that Delgadito was sure.

Preparing to step away, Ponce ran his hand along the side of the high crest muscle—that mass of hard tissues that gives to a stallion the curving reach. His hand was hidden under the heavy mane that was like coarsely-spun silver, when, half-way along the muscle, it stopped. He moved his finger tips, feeling of the oddly-shaped scar. Then, wanting to see it, he parted the mane and looked closer. His breath stopped in his throat, and the ground heaved sickeningly under his feet.

It was no scar. It was a brand!

Quite distinctly, Ponce made out the letters "ST," burned into the skin with a small iron. Ever afterwards he was to recall that moment and wonder what it was that prompted him to quickly smooth the thick mane back into place over the tell-tale marks. He did it without actually thinking about it. As he stepped away, he slid his eyes quickly around, to see if his actions had been noted by Delgadito. The man was behind him, looking into Victorio's eyes. No, he had not noticed. Only then did Ponce let his breath escape in a long, slow sigh of relief, but he did not relax. For a long time he stood quite still, thinking about his discovery. Though he tried to ignore it, the one certain explanation kept pushing its way into his brain.

Victorio belonged to someone else!

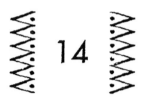

14

First Victory

FROM the moment that Ponce took a firm grip on his emotions and decided to deal firmly with Victorio, a change was noted in the stallion's attitude. There was no story-book surrender on Victorio's part, no joyous neighs ringing through the air and no begging for affection. A wild stallion never begs for anything. He will die rather than submit to the insulting touch of a human hand. From the moment he first feels a rope tighten around his neck and shut off his wind, his mind is clouded with fear and hatred for anything connected with human beings. The cloud does not suddenly float away. It hangs, dark and heavy, in the animal's brain, and when it begins to lift, the movement is so slow it is not felt nor seen by the animal. All that is known to him, finally, is that he does not fear the creatures who walk upright. He is neither surprised nor happy. He is simply unafraid.

The first part of Victorio's training ended when his eyes revealed the fact that he had learned to respect Ponce. He did not like the young man yet. He still wanted to kill him. But he admitted that his fears were perhaps not too well founded, after all, since Ponce did not strike him unless his own actions called for severe measures. His intelligence was far above that of the ordinary horse, though still far inferior to that of a man. Having been forced to depend upon his own senses for his very life, he relied more upon his senses than upon his reasoning powers. The unfamiliar was the dangerous, therefore the feared. He never questioned the warnings supplied him by his nose, his ears and his eyes. Throughout his wild life, he had respected no other creature, because he had never known any that equalled himself in strength and swiftness.

Then Ponce came into his life.

The whip came also.

All was strange.

And all was feared.

It was one of those clear, cold nights, with just enough moonlight to shed a bluish gleam over the earth and make dark shadows darker. In the blackness of the cliff's shadow, Victorio stood with head held high and nostrils dilated as he sifted the night breeze for messages. From time to time he turned, squarely facing the direction from which the wind blew. There was nothing but the scent of pines and green grass and the faint chill of snow from the distant mountains that was more a feeling than an odor. Then the wind veered, and his massive frame froze. For a long moment he stood there quivering as he drank the man smell in through his nostrils.

Gradually the mounds of muscles smoothed out under the darkly dappled coat that was a pale blue under the moon. The head lost its strained, reaching cast. There was nothing strange about those five distinct odors any more. He knew each one. It seemed now that he had always known them. He was not sure he liked them so close by, because he could not doze for more than a few minutes at a time. Still, they were harmless enough at present. He tossed his head in a high, circling movement and snorted softly. He lifted one dark leg and stamped three times in rapid succession. Finally, he set his long tail into violent circling action.

That was when Victorio stopped being afraid.

There would be many times when he would take fright at some new, disturbing thing; times when he would attempt to kill those who held him captive. But he would never again know that sickening, freezing heaviness in the pit of his stomach at the sight or scent of man.

He left the shadows, moving out across the sand with that long, elastic step of his. There was a black shadow moving with him. When he saw it, he went into the air and came down facing it. He snorted again, blowing dust high in front of his face. If a stallion can be said to dance, Victorio danced then. He stood up and walked on his hind legs, his head cocked far over as he watched his partner. He wheeled and pivoted and all but stood on his head. He ceased only when he accidentally backed into the big snubbing post.

He whirled, ready to strike out with teeth and hoofs, but when he saw it was only a post, he came out of his crouch and advanced on it. The man smell was thick here. He investigated every square inch of the pine stake, vainly trying to find something to be angry about. At last he blew upon it with his breath. It neither jumped at him nor fled from him. Even when he went up and rubbed his shoulder against it, it stayed quite firmly planted in the sand. The rubbing felt so good, he groomed his whole side, then turned and groomed the other one. At the layers of dried mud and sweat peeled off, he grunted and sighed with the sheer pleasure of it.

His hair combed, he was ready for a bath. Doubling his legs under him, he flopped over onto his side and squirmed wildly from side to side. He had forgotten all about the man smell. Suddenly the wind veered, and Victorio was on his feet in a flash, crouching and peering into the dark shadows against the far wall of the corral.

Now, of all four-legged creatures, the stallion is undoubtedly the most curious. He is worse than any child in his desire to investigate any new object and scent. He will stand for hours watching the smoke of a distant campfire, and eventually he will give in to his curiosity and go to investigate.

Victorio would have taken the prize in any contest held to determine which stallion in all the world was the most inquisitive. On soundless hoofs, he moved through the moonlight, pausing for long minutes at a time in his advance. Twice he whirled and flashed away to the safety of the shadow below the cliff, but always he came back and edged closer to the five sleeping Apaches. He was going to find out more about that Hands-and-Voice creature who persisted in running those hands over him.

For an hour he stood fifty feet from the sleeping camp, trying to make up his mind whether to flee or to attack. To his surprise, he was unable to fasten onto a reason for doing either, so he continued to stand there. He tossed his head, and the moonlight spun his thick mane into rippling silver. Well, if he didn't go over there, he would never know just how dangerous those creatures were. Yes, he especially wanted to examine the Hands-and-Voice.

He made no sound at all as he crossed the last few yards and halted at Ponce's feet. His shadow fell across the motionless form on the ground. He stood lightly-poised, ready to flee . . . or strike. He himself did not know what he would have done, if Ponce had moved then. All he did know was that there was nothing at all frightening about this slow-breathing creature below him.

His great head reached out on the thick, curved neck, and his delicate muzzle commenced to examine the worn blanket like sensitive fingers. There was the odor of wood smoke and pine and grass in the soft material. These were good odors, the kind one liked to have with one all the time. The long upper lip lifted, the big teeth closed on a fold of the blanket, and slowly Victorio drew it off the sleeping young man.

Afraid to breathe, lest he be caught at his secret game, he backed away, then turned and danced across the moonlit sand. His roving eye glimpsed his shadow again, but now it was strangely distorted by the flapping blanket in his teeth. He reared and whirled, sincerely frightened. Then the shadow disappeared behind him, and he pranced on toward the cliff. Safely hidden in the shadows, he set about the task of un-weaving the blanket. This was accomplished by the simple business of placing his forefeet squarely on it, gripping the folds firmly in his teeth and jerking his head up. The ripping cloth made a very pleasing noise in the night. He kept at his task until dawn began to tint the eastern sky. By then, the blanket was reduced to a few frayed strips of dust-covered wool.

Ponce awoke shivering. For the past hour he had slept un-easily, tossing and pulling at the blanket that seemed to have no weight and no warmth at all. The nights were always chilly up here in this high, thin atmosphere; but this was by far the coldest one he had endured. He sat up, looked around and started to roll out of his blankets. Then he stared down in surprise. There was no blanket over him! His eyes narrowed and he looked suspiciously at the four men who still slept nearby. One of them had stolen his blanket during the night! But which one? In the act of going to his hands and knees to investigate, he froze, his gaze falling on the deep hoof marks within a yard of his hands.

"*Delgadito!*"

The sleeping men jerked upright as though invisible wires had pulled them. Delgadito was on his feet, turning wildly to face whatever danger was coming, before his eyes were fully opened. When the danger did not strike nor even come within sight, he turned and glared down at Ponce.

"What you want to scare me out of ten years growth?" he snapped. "I will tie you flat on top of an ant hill."

Ponce fought to keep his face straight, but it was no easy task, considering the startling effect his call had produced. He pointed to the hoof marks in the sand. "Look," he said.

Delgadito started to mumble something about what should

be done to people with a crazy sense of humor as he squinted his sleepy eyes. "Well," he growled, "what is so interesting about horse tracks? I have seen . . ." He sucked his voice back into his throat and leaped over Ponce's head to kneel in the sand beside the tracks.

A low humming sound rolled up from his broad chest as he read the story. He straightened slowly, going to his full height and looking across the corral, which was beginning to lighten under the climbing sun. Over there against the wall, the night shadows still lay thick, but he could make out the high shape of Victorio. The stallion was standing looking toward him, and as they exchanged long glances, the horse lifted his head higher, drew a long, slow breath and released it in a loud snort. It was the first time he had done that.

Delgadito whirled, jumped back over the top of Ponce and knelt beside Joto, who was sitting on his blankets, nodding steadily. The younger man's words streamed swiftly from his lips, and The Old Apache went on nodding energetically. A moment later, Delgadito snapped a command at Juan and Dallo Chie, who had done nothing except sit and turn their heads from Ponce to Delgadito to Joto, and back again. When Delgadito yelled at them, they leaped up and commenced throwing all the camping gear onto their blankets. A moment later, they rolled the blankets tightly, swung them across their shoulders and trotted out of the corral.

Delgadito followed them more slowly, and The Old Apache turned to Ponce. "It is not certain, yet," he said in a voice which trembled slightly with hard-held excitement, "but it may be that this day is *the day*, my son. No, the wall has not fallen, but it may be shaking a little bit. We are leaving you alone with Victorio. Keep the whip in your hand at all times and do not take your eyes from him. Go to him, talk to him, study him. If it is the time, you will know it. Lead him into the stall. Do not hurry him. First, bring the bucket with a little oats in it to the stall. When he is here, maybe he will eat. If he does . . ."

He broke off, looking toward the still, shadowy form in the growing light. He studied the shape for a long moment, then grunted and followed Delgadito out of the corral.

Left alone at the stall, Ponce had a bad time of it at first. He could not seem to control his legs. They insisted on shaking like reeds in a high wind, and he could distinctly hear his teeth chattering. He was not that cold, he knew. He drew a deep breath, gripped his hands together in front of his chest and pulled with all his strength. The strain steadied him, and he sighed with relief. Now for the leap!

At the gate, he took the measure of oats Juan handed through the bars. Dumping them into the bucket, he carried them to the stall and set them down against the wall. He then picked up the long whip and started pacing toward Victorio, who had followed his every move with wide, curious eyes.

The stallion had watched the four men depart, and it bothered him rather than relieved him. This procedure was not the usual one. He did not think he liked it much. As the youth advanced slowly, he tightened his muscles, getting ready to take to his heels if anything else occurred to displease him. But the Hands-and-Voice creature sounded and acted and smelled the same as ever. For a moment, it looked as if he were going to come right on and try to do something evil, but now he had stopped. That was too bad, for without those others around, it would be an easy thing to kill this one. Victorio's chest swelled with pleasure at the exciting thought, and he stamped several times. That action had no effect on the Hands-and-Voice creature, so he snorted loudly, making the challenge unmistakably clear. Still nothing happened. Didn't the creature want to fight? Well, what *did* he want to do? Play? No, the eyes were quite steady, quite calm. The form did not move. And the voice kept going on and on, exactly as it had always done.

Victorio gave up trying to figure it out. The only thing to do was to wait and see what would happen. It was impossible to fight something that clearly had no intention of fighting. He threw his head up in that wide, swinging circle. If this upright creature didn't understand *that*, they might just as well call off the whole thing here and now!

But Ponce did understand that movement of the big head. As plainly as spoken words it said, "Well, don't just *stand* there! *Do* something!"

With his eyes fastened on the stallion's, Ponce bent and picked up the lead rope. "Come you, Victorio," he commanded, tugging gently. "We will go to the stall, and you will enter it without acting crazy. I have the whip today, so you had better not start thinking about pounding me into the ground! Try that, you big goat, and I will skin you alive and make you into a pair of pants! Come you. I am going to take hold of your halter, and we are going to walk side by side for a change. Come you big goat!"

For a moment Victorio pretended he did not know what the tugging on his halter meant. He stood perfectly still, letting his head see-saw up and down with the pull, then he lifted a forefoot and set it down a mere six inches ahead of the other. The voice continued to flow around his small pointed ears, and he began to twitch those ears in an effort to sift every shade and tone for some hidden meaning. He could find nothing at all to be alarmed about, which was slightly disappointing, so he lifted the other forefoot and set it down six inches ahead of the first. This half-advance went on until he was stretched out so far he began to wobble slightly. He was obliged to move a hind foot to keep from falling. That was very risky. He snorted at his own courage.

His ears were twitching faster and faster. There must be some hint in that voice as to what was going to happen. It did not change by so much as a half-tone. Well, this was amazing indeed! There was some trick to it, that much was certain. It had never happened before, therefore it was not to be trusted.

The small ears suddenly flattened, shutting out the voice. The dark legs moved more quickly, took longer steps, and a moment later Ponce was forced to tilt his head far back in order to keep his gaze on the wide eyes above him. His every nerve was strung to tightly he knew he could not move, even if his life depended on it, which it well might. Fixing his whole mind on the simple act, he reached up and grasped the chin strap of the hackamore. The head seemed to be set in concrete. The wide nostrils were pinched in and wrinkled, and the ears were almost hidden in the glistening mane. Plainly Victorio was placing no trust whotsoever in this new procedure. One wrong move on his part, the young man knew, could turn the giant gray into a raging killer. He knew also that he would be unable to escape, if that happened. Those sharp forefeet could strike with the deadly accuracy of a rattler.

"Victorio," he ordered, "put those ears up where they belong! And quit curling up your nose as though you smelled a skunk! Maybe I don't smell like a horse, but I don't smell *that* bad either. Now, when I say, 'Walk!' we start toward the stall. You hear? Remember you: I have this whip, and if you get crazy, I will brain you, you old goat! Now . . . *walk!*"

For one endless moment it seemed that Victorio was not going to obey the voice and the pressure on his hackamore. Then, he released a loud snort, shook his head so violently he almost tore the hackamore from Ponce's grip and stepped forward. A half dozen steps onward, his ears flipped erect, then slanted sharply forward. He tossed his head again, lifting Ponce off the ground. So this, his actions stated clearly, was all there was to it! His body lost its stiff action, his tail lifted, and he began to walk with high, springy steps.

Halfway to the stall, a particularly vigorous toss of the stallion's head swung Ponce a foot off the ground. Startled, he spoke loudly, and the tone knifed through Victorio's lightly-balanced mind and was interpreted as a warning of danger.

He reared, shook Ponce off and wheeled away. Eyes starting in terror, he took three lunging strides before the rope tightened. He skidded to an abrupt halt and faced about. He had learned the futility of fighting that rope.

"Victorio!" Ponce called sternly. "Come you back here! I did not even touch you. It was your own head-throwing that scared you. I am not made of bricks, and I cannot keep my feet on the ground, if you pull me into the air, can I? Come you, silly goat!"

The stallion was still trembling from his scare. It required another half hour to again bring him within reach. Once more, the pair started for the stall, and once more the stallion's own playfulness and strength resulted in his taking fright and bolting. To the patient Ponce, time stood still. Nothing mattered except getting the gray into the stall without employing force.

When Victorio reared and lunged away for the third time, the young Apache lifted the whip and caught him on the rump with the tip. It was not a cutting blow. It barely stung the thick hide, but its effect was instantaneous and wholly satisfactory. In mid-stride Victorio grunted, stiffened his legs and plowed to a stop. The look he turned on Ponce clearly said, "Now, how did *that* happen?"

He came to the young man more quickly this time, all too anxious to avoid a second mysterious pinching on his rear end. It was beginning to look as if one could do nothing without this creature's knowing about it beforehand! At the stall, another hour was spent with the stallion blowing and snorting over every square inch of the structure. He acted as if he had never seen the thing before. But eventually his curiosity triumphed over his uneasiness, and he allowed himself to be led into it. Immediately, he changed his mind and shot back out, and the whole sniffing, blowing and snorting process had to be repeated.

When the stallion was again inside, Ponce took a half dozen quick turns around the snubbing post with the rope.

He had become unbelievably tired, all at once. Something warned him that he had better bring the thing to a close very quickly. He had not been aware of anything except the stallion from the moment he had first spoken to him. Now he glanced up and saw that the sun was over three hours high! He tried to remember where it had been when he had started toward Victorio, but it was becoming increasingly difficult to think clearly. When he stepped away from the post, he stumbled. Vaguely he realized that his nerves had been strained to fever pitch too long. It was the same feeling that came over him after a race, only worse. All his muscles were turning to jelly, and he had trouble focusing his eyes.

He staggered to the corner of the stall and reached up to stroke the damp neck where the hairs formed a cowlick at the base of the heavy jaws. The motion was never completed. Without warning, his legs buckled under him. He grabbed for the logs, but he could not pull himself up. He saw Victorio's eyes on him and saw the question in them, but when he tried to speak, his lips refused to move. With a low moan, he reeled against the logs, slipped lower and fell over onto his back as soft blackness rolled over him.

15

No Quarter!

IT WAS a month before David Forrest returned to the mountain valley, instead of a week. Upon his return to Shady Mesa, he was called east by a horse breeder who had two yearlings he thought the Arizona horseman might fancy. No sooner had David Forrest contracted for their delivery, than a call came from California. He promptly flew to the west coast, where he engaged in further horse trading. Since he never considered making a purchase without the advice of Gil Dreen and Joe Marino, the three of them were absent from Arizona nearly three weeks. Then they were obliged to await the arrival of their purchases, and another seven days slipped by.

Though still in Arizona, Gabe Stuart was as effectively prevented from leaving his ranch as he would have been had he been bound hand and foot. He took care of his cattle without the aid of a rider, and as luck would have it, the fences chose that particular time to go down in countless places, and the ditches clogged up and overflowed their banks. All of which made a very busy man of the rancher.

It was exactly one month to the day from the time they had jumped into truck and pick-up and set off on the wild horse hunt that the same five again started the trip into the mountains.

Ponce had looked for his friends each day, but when the days stretched into weeks with no sign of them, he realized that their own interests were preventing their immediate return. Knowing they would come when they could, he kept his thoughts on the business of converting Victorio into a believer in the goodness of mankind.

It was not an easy task. At times it appeared well nigh impossible. He had been fooled into thinking the gray's acceptance of him that one morning indicated a sudden about-face of the stallion's attitude, especially when the animal had just stood quietly by until he recovered from his momentary blackout from sheer exhaustion. He could not have been more wrong had he believed that the moon was made of green cheese. To all appearances, Victorio had simply used that morning for the purpose of storing up more strength for continued resistance.

For ten days it was necessary for the three grown men and Ponce to use every trick known to wild horse runners in order to fight Victorio into the stall and keep him there. During those struggles, the valley again rang with the vicious animal's insane screams and bellows, and the heavy sand of the corral was pounded to powdery whiteness by the plunging hoofs and racing feet. The thing began to take on the aspects of an endless nightmare.

None of his companions seemed to share Ponce's uneasiness. In fact, Joto was plainly pleased. "He is himself again," he informed the bewildered boy. "That time he wanted to be friends with you, he was not himself. One day he will be like that all the time, maybe, but now he must work his wildness and his meanness out in his own way. In time he will decide there is no point in fighting, and he will want to be friends with you again. It is his way. You cannot change it."

Three weeks from the day Victorio had been captured Juan lugged his heavy stock saddle into the corral and dumped it onto the ground, squarely under the surprised animal's nose.

Mid-morning came and with it a gradual lessening of the stallion's uneasiness at this new turn of events. He lowered his head and sucked the oiled-leather scent deep into his lungs. After an hour of minute inspection, he flipped his ears forward, signifying his acceptance of the new article.

Immediately, Delgadito spoke to Juan and Dallo Chie, who came over and began to remove one log from either side of the stall. The logs were fixed to the corner posts with rawhide thongs and could be removed individually. The two which the men removed were on a level with the stallion's chest, and for some time Ponce was kept in ignorance as to the purpose of their being taken away. He stood talking to Victorio while his companions went about the business they knew so well.

When Dallo Chie was in place on the opposite side of the stall, Juan lifted the big saddle. Dallo Chie caught it, and the two of them held it a foot above Victorio's back. Slowly they lowered it until the fleece padding brushed the gray shoulders, and there they held it while the stallion proceeded to show them how little he took to the idea of wearing one of those contraptions.

A quarter hour passed before the crazed struggles lessened. The saddle was lowered again, more firmly this time, at which a second hysterical outburst on the part of the stallion held up the proceedings another quarter hour. When the gear came down for the third time, it was not lifted. It was held in place on the heaving, twisting back until that back settled to a level line.

Victorio stood crouched under the strange article, his whole body quivering and streaming with sweat. Clearly he expected pain with every racing second. When it did not come, his trembling gradually lessened, then stopped altogether. The rigid mounds of muscles smoothed out, and again the mountain stallion released that long, unsteady breath that sounded like a sigh.

"We will not tighten the cinch," said Delgadito. "It is enough for now that he bears the saddle quietly. We leave it on him and go away. Ponce, stay you here and try to talk some sense into his head."

Juan started away, then he turned and shouted, "You don't let that stud get my saddle down in that stall and pound it to pieces, you hear me?"

Ponce moved one hand in an affirmative gesture and smiled as Dallo Chie slapped his friend on the back and took out at a dead run for the gate. The Old Apache and Delgadito followed more slowly. The corral was empty except for Victorio and his constant companion.

At noon, Delgadito brought the youth a piece of roasted venison. "How goes it, brother?" he asked, running his glance over the quiet stallion. "He does not try to get Juan's saddle under his hoofs?"

Ponce shook his head, unable to speak because his mouth was full of venison.

"Good!" Delgadito grinned. "Juan is worried about it. He says if Victorio wrecks it, he is going to skin him and have a new one made from his hide."

Ponce nodded this time, his eyes showing his amusement at the idea. The tall man turned and strolled away. He paused and called over his shoulder, "I think maybe I will go for a ride to the lake. Will you shoot me if I ride your Desert Storm?"

Still chewing, Ponce shook his head, and the other exclaimed, "Good! I have never sat on what you call a Thoroughbred. Maybe I will make a trade with you, if I think she is better than my cayuse."

Ponce managed to mumble the Apache equivalent of

"Don't say!" and shook his fist at his friend, who laughed
and vaulted over the high gate. Ten minutes later, the chains
of that gate rattled, and Ponce glanced up to see Delgadito
appear astride Desert Storm. He choked and gulped the meat
down, his eyes almost popping from his head. What did that
man think he was doing, bringing a filly into the corral with
Victorio!

He laid both hands on the rope and began to mumble
swiftly. "Now Victorio! Now Victorio! Don't explode! Desert
Storm is coming to visit you—plague on that Delgadito—She
is a very fine filly—may Delgadito have bad dreams—And
she will tell you how pleasant it is to be ridden by a man—
I would strangle that Delgadito, if I could—So don't explode!"

Desert Storm was nervous from the moment she stepped
through the gateway. She moved with short, half-rearing
bounds, her legs bunched under her. A dozen yards into the
corral, she turned and flirted sideways, then bounced up and
down on stiffened forelegs. Sweat began to glisten on her neck
and shoulders, and she kept trying to rear.

Ponce turned from watching her to see Victorio crouching
low in the stall, as if preparing to leap over it. He was quivering in every muscle. His thick neck swelled with the tightened
muscles, and the heavy juglar vein pulsed faster and faster as
the filly's scent was carried to him on the breeze. It had been
a long time since he had last been close to one of his own
kind. His mares had all but slipped from their place in his
thoughts. But here was a new mare! She was tall and black and
graceful—like the deer which sometimes came into the valley
to feed with the band. She was coming closer . . . closer. . . .
Her breath ran along his flank, and the touch of it was like
the warming winds of spring after the icy blasts of winter.
Then it was on his shoulder. It was caressing his own face.
He turned his head and fixed his amazed gaze on the soft,
dark eyes. His explosive grunt was like a joyful shout, and

Delgadito laughed as he held the black filly close to the stall.

Victorio had fallen hopelessly in love!

His eyes were not flat and blank now. They were glowing with a light Ponce had never seen in them, and an instant later, the stallion reached out and nipped the filly's neck gently. He did not move as she half reared, squealed, and struck out angrily with her right forefoot. But he did not nip her lovingly again. Quite clearly she had given him to understand she was as taken with this meeting as he was.

Feeling herself to be mistress of the situation, Desert Storm consented to having the side of her neck nuzzled, and when her suitor assured her he would not dream of offending her a second time, she turned her head toward him. For long minutes they stood with muzzles touching, talking in that silent language which is more eloquent than spoken words. When Delgadito reined Desert Storm away, she moved reluctantly, turning her head back to keep her new-found acquaintance in sight.

"Now the work will be made easier, maybe," Delgadito said with great satisfaction, holding the filly to a stand a dozen yards away. "Each time your old stud is in the stall, or safely held with the rope, we will let Desert Storm talk to him some more. Maybe she can convince him that life is not all ugliness."

As the filly moved toward the gate, Victorio kept his gaze on her. When she was out of sight, he gave voice to a shrill neigh of loneliness that climbed into the still air and quivered out across the valley. An answering call sounded from beyond the pines, and that, naturally demanded a second neigh on Victorio's part. The horse-shouts went back and forth at regular intervals until the filly was far up the valley.

Victorio snorted and shook his head impatiently when Ponce touched him, then he turned and began nuzzling the logs against which Desert Storm's body had rubbed. For a half hour he continued to inhale the sweet scent left there.

When Ponce commenced stroking the damp neck, there was no resistance on the part of the gray.

The young Apache lifted the heavy saddle to the ground, loosened the rope and stood back to let Victorio leave the stall in the customary way—like a bolt of lightning. But the stallion did not whirl and bolt to the far side of the corral this time. He was giving all his attention to Ponce, who had on him the scent of the filly. When the rope tugged beneath his chin, he obeyed without hesitation. And when one of the hands rose to scratch him behind the ears, he cocked his head to one side and lowered it. The closer his muzzle came to the creature, the thicker became the scent of the filly. And so it was that the graceful Desert Storm accomplished in short minutes what four grown men and a youth had failed to accomplish in weeks.

Ponce kept his voice steady with an effort. "Victorio," he informed the stallion, "you are not quite as wild as you thought you were, maybe. Now you and I are going to walk around this corral. When I say 'Walk!' we walk. When I say, 'Trot!' we trot. Remember that. Come you, now. Walk!"

They started off at a fairly reasonable pace, but before long the stallion began to reach his legs out in what was for him a casual walk. For Ponce it was a matter of trotting or being dragged off his feet. So he trotted while Victorio walked. By the time they had circled the corral three times, he was gasping for breath. The stallion, showing no such signs of fatigue, began to toss his head up and down, which action resulted in Ponce's being pulled into the air every twenty feet or so. His right arm began to feel like a wet rag, so, with a loud gasp, he called, "Whoa!" and stumbled to a halt.

It required fully ten minutes for him to regain his breath. "Victorio," he stated, "your legs are too long for this—or mine are too short. I am going to turn loose your halter and hold onto the rope. We will now trot . . . slowly!"

He set off again, but instead of jogging as he had intended

doing, he found himself going at a dead run. At the agency school he had been considered extremely fleet of foot, but he soon realized that a man's legs were never meant to keep stride with a horse's. Foot by foot, he fell behind the stallion, and when he gripped the rope tighter, he was pulled along in great, soaring strides.

"Hey, you Victorio!" he choked. "Stop! Whoa!"

He started to lean back and stiffen his legs—and promptly found himself hauled along on his stomach in Victorio's dust. He twisted and turned and fell headlong a dozen times before he finally succeeded in regaining his feet. "Whoa!" he commanded sternly. Victorio trotted on, deaf to the command which he in all probability never heard. He was enjoying himself more and more. Only when the nose band of the hackamore banged sharply against his nose did he pull up short. He slid to a stop and looked around at his dust-mantled, gasping companion, as if to ask what came next.

"You—you are too much horse for—for me!" Ponce panted, clutching his side to ease the pain burning there. "We —we will go and rest by the stall. Come you." He walked across the hot sand, his legs threatening to collapse at every step. Reaching the stall, he flung himself full length on the ground and gulped the thin, clear air hungrily.

Victorio stood over him, his ears flicking back and forth as he sifted the breeze for strange sounds. He could find nothing to be alarmed about, so after awhile he let his head droop, closed his eyes and dozed. Twice he wakened and stood staring at the still figure on the ground in front of him. Twice the thought flashed through his brain that he could in all probability rear and drive the sleeping figure into the sand without suffering any pain from that black, snake-like rope. But the scent of the filly was still heavy in the air. There seemed to be no danger in this sleeping creature. And so he let the thought depart, sighed gently and dozed on.

Bright and early the next morning, Delgadito came to the stall and announced matter-of-factly, "We will saddle him. You will then ride him."

Ponce opened his mouth, then closed it without saying anything. His legs were beginning to feel like wet rags again, so he held onto the snubbing post until they ceased shaking. By the time The Old Apache, Juan and Dallo Chie were present, he had gained control of himself sufficiently to be able to let loose of the post and take his place at Victorio's head.

There was a visible tremor throughout the big frame in the stall as the heavy stock saddle was lowered by Juan and Dallo Chie. But no such violent explosion as the one of the previous day followed the first part of the saddling routine. As the cinch was passed under the deep chest, a dark hind leg struck out twice. Still, the stallion offered no real resistance.

"Now," said Delgadito, "get up there, brother. Put one foot on each wall and lower yourself very slowly into the saddle. When you are ready, nod to me, and I will untie him and throw you the rope."

With his stomach turning somersaults, Ponce obeyed silently. He grabbed the top log, drew himself up and straddled the stall, one foot firmly planted on each top log. Beneath him, the stallion stood as still as stone, his ears erect, his eyes rolled far back in their sockets. Inch by inch, the young man lowered himself until his knees touched the hard, shining leather. There he crouched, waiting for the eruption that was sure to come. Victorio did not move—did not even move his ears by so much as a half inch. But as Ponce grasped the horn and started to remove his feet from the logs, the stallion began to sink away under him. He crouched as low as he could, and, with the sinking of his body, his ears flattened, his nostrils widened, and his tail was tucked tightly against the dappled rump. But he did not struggle, even when Ponce eased into the saddle and bore all his weight on it.

Minute after minute, the waiting silence held. Very slowly,

Ponce reached a hand down and stroked the rigid shoulder in front of his knee. There was no flicker of movement under his palm. He flashed a look toward Delgadito, then nodded ever so slightly. The man took a length of rope, knotted both ends to the chin strap of the hackamore and gently passed the rope over Victorio's head to Ponce.

Slowly, almost carelessly. Delgadito loosened the long tie rope from the snubbing post. His eyes were fixed on Victorio's left shoulder, and when he saw the muscles knot and tighten, he flipped the lead rope off the post and flung it to Ponce.

The young Apache made a wild grab, caught the coils and lifted both legs high, to avoid having them crushed as Victorio shot out of the stall. That first backward motion halted abruptly. There was one split second of complete motionlessness. Then, before he was completely set, Ponce felt the saddle drop from under him and tip crazily as Victorio went to one side in a crouching, twisting leap. His slim body snapped like a whip as the stallion stuck his head between his legs and kicked at the sky, then whirled and tried to climb into that same sky. When the lithe, swaying form did not shoot out of the saddle, the stallion threw himself into a series of those murderous leaps and twists and whirls that give professional horse-breakers nightmares.

Again and again, the massive gray shot into the air and came down on stiffened legs with a force that jarred the ground, and washed all color from Ponce's strained face. Failing in that, the stallion started that most dangerous of all tricks, the whirling buck. With his hind feet moving no more than a yard in any direction, he spun in a tight circle to the left, then reversed directions while his rider was off balance. He came out of that with a rolling, whipping twist that lifted the saddle three inches off his back and threw his rider down across the horn with sickening force.

Stars blazed before Ponce's eyes, his breath was knocked out of him, and he began to bleed through the nose. He lost a stirrup, kicked frantically to retrieve it and caught it barely in time to avoid being flung a dozen feet into the air by the stallion's sunfishing jump that pointed the four stiffened legs toward the sky, then wrenched the lathered body straight as the ground rose. The dark legs buckled, and, in a choking, spurting cloud of dust, horse and rider crashed down.

Automatically, Ponce rolled out of the saddle as the gray fell, but he grabbed the horn and let the stallion's rising lunge fling him once more astride. There had long since ceased to be any such thing as time, and as the battle raged back and forth across the corral, the young Apache began to lose consciousness. The maddened shrieks and squeals of the animal under him faded steadily, until he was riding a whirlwind that spun him faster and faster into a soundless void. He tried to call to Delgadito to rope the stallion, but, as he opened his mouth, his head was snapped back and his teeth sank deeply into his tongue. He could no longer see the ground nor the walls of the valley—not even the sky. All that was visible through the billowing dust were the lathered shoulders and the whipping, silvery mane of his mount. The front of the saddle tipped until the horn struck him in the stomach, dropped away and rolled to one side. There was one last convulsive twist, one last soaring leap, and then the stallion surged forward in a dead run, straight for the gate!

In terror, Ponce leaned far to one side and attempted to pull the crazed animal away, but no human hands could turn Victorio. Ponce gripped the steel-like coils of the lead rope and slashed at the extended head with superhuman strength. Less than fifty feet separated them from the gate when the stallion veered to the left and streaked along the bottom of the fence.

The rampaging animal held to the run four times around the corral. He sank to his fetlocks in the sand at every stride, and before long the dragging weight of that sand forced him to slow down. On the fifth circle, he broke and began to labor, but the heavy coils in the rider's hand struck him across the shoulder, and he again flung himself into a run. He slowed to a trot less than a hundred yards onward, and after that he did not respond to the urging rope. Twenty feet from the stall, he planted his feet wide and halted, with his head almost touching the sand. He was weaving on his feet, and his darkly dappled coat was white with lather.

Reeling in the saddle, Ponce clutched the horn with both hands and fought to keep from tumbling to the ground. The corral was spinning and dipping before his eyes. He could hear nothing at all, and his insides felt as if they had turned to jelly. Slowly, he pulled his feet from the stirrups and leaned down, but suddenly his fingers slipped off the horn and he plunged toward the sand. He felt strong hands catch him and break his fall. From a great distance, he heard a voice which sounded vaguely like Delgadito's, but when he tried to stand, he found he had no legs at all, and he slumped helplessly in his friend's arms. Even the strongest of constitutions—and will to conquer—could not help but yield temporarily to the series of superhuman tests that this boy had been enduring.

With agonizing slowness, the world stopped spinning. Ponce managed to stiffen his legs so that they would support him. He said faintly, "Let me go, Delgadito," and reached up to grasp Victorio's hackamore.

"Come you," he whispered. "Walk!"

Staggering with every slow step, horse and rider reached the stall, and when Ponce croaked a command, the stallion walked in between the walls. The young Apache started to unbuckle the cinch strap, but he pitched forward, cracking his head against one of the logs, nor could he struggle to his feet to complete the task he had started. "Delgadito," he croaked, trying to focus his blood-shot eyes on the tall rider who had never left his side, "maybe you had better do it." He waited until the man nodded and moved to comply, then let himself slide down the wall until he was sitting on the sand. He managed a wan smile as Delgadito laid the saddle aside and squatted down beside him. "I rode him, did I not?" he asked.

"You rode him, brother," Delgadito said quietly. "Maybe one day you show me how it is done, no?"

"This makes twice I have ridden him," Ponce whispered. "If the third time is to be worse than this one, I think maybe one of us will give up."

Delgadito did not reply to that immediately. He nodded to himself several times. "Maybe," he murmured finally, "maybe that stud has decided it won't be you who gives up."

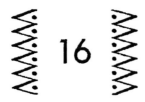

16

The Heart of a Thoroughbred

NEVER again did Victorio buck.

It was as if that one murderous battle had torn the last shreds of hatred from his mind. He became quiet—though by no means gentle. He ceased struggling against the ropes at the entrance to the stall, and his burly form no longer shrank and quivered at the touch of the saddle. No day passed that he did not strike at Ponce or one of the men, but at the touch of the quirt—the lash had been taken out of the corral and permanently stored among The Old Apache's belongings—he straightened, as though anxious to do what was expected of him.

This willingness of his posed something of a problem, both for horse and handlers. Invariably he did a thing too quickly and with far too much energy. If it was a matter of reining to the right, he whirled like a cutting horse, instead of like the big animal he was. If he was going at a slow canter and the hackamore indicated he was to stop, he jammed all four feet into the ground and instantly froze into a statue. This sudden halting resulted in Ponce's being flung flat over the saddle horn. After numerous repetitions of it, the youth's stomach began to turn a dark blue tone.

Instead of moving from a stand into a slow walk at the

touch of the spurs, the stallion leaped into a dead run with the uncoiling motion of a released spring. Instead of cantering in a wide, slow circle, he leaned so sharply inward that Ponce's stirrup all too often brushed the sand. He could not travel at a collected canter. If the reins slackened so much as a quarter inch, he was immediately sprinting full out, and to sit that streaking gray in a high run was to know the feeling of being flung, helpless, into the funnel of a whirlwind.

Accustomed to the feel of Desert Storm's comparatively slender build, Ponce had difficulty getting the feel of Victorio. The back was a good deal broader and it was heavily corded with those long, rolling muscles which can lift a stallion onto his hind legs and hold him erect for an amazingly long time. When tensed, those same muscles can roll a tightly cinched saddle from side to side as if the gear were not held down at all. Experiencing that lifting, rolling motion repeatedly, Ponce realized that his control over the stallion depended wholly upon his own unceasing alertness and upon the gray's willingness to obey the firm hands and equally firm voice.

One more fact was brought home to Ponce. A stallion is incapable of relaxing. The ears move as if attached to the head on swivel hinges, forever flicking back and forth, individually or in unison, forever sifting the air for new sounds. The nostrils keep time with the ears, flaring, twitching, and wrinking, testing the breezes for telltale scents. The eyes are never still in their sockets, and the head moves back and forth and up and down. Even in sleep, the ears do not droop, but stand stiffly at attention, ready to warn the sleeper of approaching danger.

These things Ponce learned through experience and through the words of The Old Apache, who instructed him by the hour on the habits and peculiarities of that noblest of all four-legged creatures—the stallion. Each time he ended his lecture with: "You must never forget this, and you must never trust Victorio. Not until you *know* he is speaking the truth when he says to you, 'I will not harm you.'"

Only once did Ponce voice the question that was uppermost in his mind. "Why did he stop bucking after the one time?"

The Old Apache grunted. "You will know in time, my son. I know, but the proof is only in my head, and so I will not tell you." He gave his young companion a half-smile, then sobered. "This you remember: When our white friends return, there will be great danger, maybe. Have always the spurs on your boots and the quirt in your hand. You will have to use them with all your strength or Victorio will kill that beautiful Iron Duke, if they bring him with them. Know you that." He saw a shadow come into the wide, dark eyes of his young companion and pointed a bony forefinger sternly. "You think you will hurt Victorio? Ha! The spurs and the whip will be like the sting of bees on his tough hide, nothing more. You cannot hurt him. You can but sting him so fast and in so many places, he will want to run instead of fight."

"Those spurs are sharp," Ponce said hesitantly.

"And Victorio's hide is tough and thick!" Joto snapped. "A man who cannot bring himself to master a stallion has no right to possess one! Does your heart grow soft within you again?"

Ponce moved his head from side to side. "No, my father," he replied quietly. "I will use the spurs and the quirt, if it has to be."

"Look you," the ancient warrior said in a kinder tone. "Even if those spurs of Delgadito's which you use were Mexican 'Cutting Hooks,' they would not hurt Victorio very much. In the first place, your legs have not the strength to drive them in too deeply, and in the second place, that hide of his has a thick layer of leathery muscles under it. You dig in with the spurs, and they bounce out, do they not?" When the youth nodded, he said quietly, "All right then, do not hesitate to use those spurs when it is necessary. If they hurt him, you would know it quickly enough. Know you that."

For two days Victorio had been taken out of the corral and exercised along the valley wall, in the company of Desert

Storm. Delgadito rode the black filly and kept a firm grip on the stallion's lead rope, in case the stallion decided to throw his rider and take out for the upper end of the valley, where his mares grazed.

The precaution was entirely unnecessary. Victorio was far too interested in the tall filly to think of escaping. Tail erect, chin tucked in until it touched his broad chest, he danced along in a manner to excite envy in the most beautifully trained show horse. It was almost laughable—the way he paraded for his aloof companion's benefit.

Twice during these afternoon outings, Delgadito lifted Desert Storm into a reaching canter, holding her from a run with some difficulty. As Victorio moved to match her strides, Ponce could hardly restrain a shout of sheer joy at the almost frightening power of the gray under him. In this swifter motion, there was no hint of heaviness, and the long dark legs had the effortless, floating action of a blooded racer. Acutely aware of the as yet untried strength of Victorio, he wondered what would happen if these two animals were matched against each other in a race.

Such a race, he knew, would not be a fair test of the stallion's speed, for though he moved without strain or awkwardness, he had not yet born a saddle and rider long enough to have gained the perfect balance which would come in time. Moreover, the weight of the heavy saddle and Ponce was of definite importance, since they were at present much heavier on the animal who had never carried anything except himself than they would be, once he found his legs.* It would be a handicap with the rules reversed, one in which the untried labored under added poundage while the proved winner ran with empty pockets.**

* A way of saying a horse moves equally freely and easily under saddle and rider as he does alone.
** The lead weights used in Handicaps are assigned to the horses according to age, sex, working time and number of wins within a given period, on the theory that such weights will render all animals in the race equal.

On the third day, Ponce took the stallion out alone, a thing to which Victorio objected strongly. He carried himself proudly as before; but he repeatedly attempted to rear and return to the grove and Desert Storm. Ponce was obliged to use the spurs throughout the first half hour, but gradually the stallion quieted and threw himself into his work with his customary energy.

In an effort to train the gray to work in a collected manner, Ponce rode in a circle some hundred yards in diameter. They went at a walk the first half dozen times, then Ponce said, "Trot" and gave the reins a gentle shake. As Victorio lunged into a run, Ponce threw his weight back, hauled hard on the rope reins and clapped the spurs into the muscle-cushioned ribs. The stallion knew exactly what those stinging thrusts meant. They meant *stop!* He stiffened his legs and sat down and Ponce was rocked forward against the high front swell of the stock saddle.

Victorio did not move until the spurs released him. Then he snorted and stamped, impatient to repeat the process. The circling continued by leaps and starts and skidding halts for an hour. Ponce's face and bare back were streaming, and sweat glistened on Victorio's shoulders and flanks. The rider was much the tireder of the two.

A sound coming down from the top of the wall drew Ponce's attention upward. The next instant, he was waving to Gabe Stuart, who was closely followed by Joe Marino on The Iron Duke. The instant after that, the young Apache was fighting to drag Victorio out of the dead run into which the unexpected movement of his hand had flung the nervous stallion. He was well over two hundred yards away from the wall by the time he managed to turn the excited animal and pull him in, and by that time the five white hunters had descended into the valley and started out to meet him. What happened a moment later was forever afterwards a nightmare in Ponce's memory.

He saw Joe Marino ride out ahead of the others, and then the world went crazy. The usually calm Iron Duke caught the wild stallion's scent on the wind. The threat to his own life was instantly sensed by him, though he had never had occasion to defend himself against the rigidly controlled colts in the racing world. Once a half-mad stable mate had attacked him, but the fight had been halted before he had been given time to realize what was happening. Now he instinctively hurled a challenge at the distant stallion, and when an answering shriek pierced the still air, he grabbed the bit in his jaws and streaked forward.

Ponce's first warning of tragedy came to him as the massive gray rose, screaming, to flail the air with his forefeet, then crashed down and bolted straight for the oncoming Iron Duke. The youth clutched wildly at the horn to keep from being thrown from the hurtling body. He caught his balance and raked the bulging shoulders with the spurs the while he sawed on the rope reins with all his strength. He might as well have attempted to drag Gabe Stuart's adobe house off its foundation with a string.

The running stallions approached each other like flashing shadows. The distance between them narrowed from two hundred yards to a hundred and fifty . . . one hundred . . . seventy-five. With awful clearness, Ponce could see the killing light in The Iron Duke's staring eyes. In the far distance he heard voices shouting back and forth, and caught a fleeting glimpse of Barbara Forrest trying to bring Last Laugh up on The Iron Duke. He saw Joe Marino using his whip on the racer with desperate violence and without any effect. He did not see Desert Storm, with Delgadito astride her back, flash out of the trees a half mile away and start toward him at a high run.

Numb with terror, he lifted the heavy coil of lead rope and slashed Victorio alongside the head in an attempt to make him veer aside. The stallion did not waver. His mind was locked on a single idea—murder! Deaf and blind and completely insensitive to pain, he streaked on, his wicked head aimed straight for The Iron Duke's throat.

In the instant before the two big animals collided, Ponce flung all his weight to the left—and saw Joe Marino lean in the opposite direction. As if guided by the same muscles, the two riders hauled their mounts' heads around at a cramped angle, and then the stallions came together with a force that drove their wind out in twin gusts and knocked them reeling apart.

Off balance, Victorio stumbled and crashed onto his left side. He ploughed a furrow in the grassy turf for twenty feet. His skidding fall jarred his second shriek out of him, and, as he threshed and lunged to his feet, Ponce miraculously succeeded in regaining his own feet and making a flying leap for the saddle horn. He caught it, and Victorio's whirling lunge jerked him into the saddle. He was whipped far to one side as the gray crouched and wheeled away to dodge the throw Gabe Stuart made with his lasso. The loop fell short. With a deafening scream, Victorio rose, then came down and crouched to hurl himself forward in a second slashing attack.

The Iron Duke had not fallen, but he had been jarred off balance. For fifty yards he stumbled on, trying to wrench the reins out of his rider's hands. Failing in that, he reared and spun. Before he could gather himself, the heavy butt of the jockey's whip caught him between the ears. The shock of the blow jerked him back to sanity. For one single instant he stood facing the murderous Victorio, stark terror knifing through him. Then the whip cut him across the rump and he wheeled and fled. Within a dozen yards, he was reaching for his full, graceful racing stride.

The Iron Duke was through with fighting, but Victorio was not. With one convulsive movement of his gigantic body, he launched himself in pursuit of the frightened racer.

Ponce was sobbing with frustration and rage. He yelled into the flattened ears, and repeatedly lashed at the out-thrust head with the coiled rope. He screamed in blind terror as he caught a glimpse of Barbara coming in at an angle, to cut between Victorio and The Iron Duke.

He tried to swing Victorio away, then abandoned the attempt as he saw the chestnut filly falter in mid-stride, slow, and plunge away in fright.

The ground was a green blur under Victorio's thundering hoofs. Ponce could not breathe. The wind pushed at him like a smothering hand, and his eyes streamed as the whipping silver mane stung them like countless darting flames. Through a swirling mist, he caught a glimpse of The Iron Duke, fifty yards in the lead. He knew that colt, and because he knew him, he felt a wild hope leap to life as his eyes told him that the racer had gone into his top stride. Like a bird skimming low over the ground, the sleek Forrest Thoroughbred was running his best under the insistent whip of Joe Marino. If he could hold that lead! If he could outrun Victorio this time . . . !

He could not. Foot by foot, yard by yard, his lead was cut down. Ponce stared in disbelief. No horse in the world could catch The Iron Duke—not with over fifty yards to make up! And then he knew what had happened.

Terrified beyond belief, the Thoroughbred was not running with his customary balance. His action was rough, his strides far shorter than usual. In a state of shock, he could not pull his attention from the danger closing in on his rear and fix it on what he was doing—running for his life. With sickening swiftness, the beautiful colt was going down before the wild gray's challenge. Less than a dozen yards stretched between his streaming tail and Victorio's red-lined nostrils . . . six yards. He fought to regain his lead; but it was too late—or was it? From some hidden well of reserve, The Iron Duke drew one last ounce of strength and managed somehow to keep those flaring nostrils at his flank.

A shout was whipped along the wind, and Ponce turned to see Delgadito coming in on his left. Huddled up along her churning shoulders, the Apache was riding Desert Storm like a jockey. There was no saddle nor bridle on the filly. She ran in obedience to the hands of her rider. And she ran as she had never run before. Even with fear clutching at him with icy fingers, Ponce could not but marvel at his filly's breathtaking speed. He had never before seen her in action with a rider on her back. Now he watched her turn a hundred feet away and start her move against Victorio.

For one instant he saw her falter as she came out of her turn, but the next instant she was coming on with everquickening strides. He glanced ahead, saw The Iron Duke holding his place a half length ahead, then whirled back to watch Desert Storm. A low cry that was never heard issued from his throat as realization of what this meant swept over him.

Desert Storm was being matched against Victorio!

Whether the big filly realized the deadly urgency for speed, or whether she was running for the sheer joy of running, only she knew. Whatever her reasons, she set herself to the task of catching the two stallions with a cold and deadly determination that hurled her over the ground with dazzling swiftness.

In the opening sprint, before she had fully recovered from that single faltering stride, she fell back a dozen yards. Then she steadied and began to move up remorselessly. With her long body stretched low, her delicate legs an invisible blur, she appeared to Ponce fully extended; but as Delgadito lifted a hand and slapped her on her right shoulder, he saw that he had been mistaken. She responded with a second burst of speed that made Ponce's eyes widen in astonishment. Inch by inch, her strides lengthened, quickened, became one long, motionless blur. She was three lengths behind Victorio. When she hung there for a dozen strides, Delgadito's hand again brushed her churning shoulder, and she again responded to that touch.

Ponce saw that final supreme effort she made to draw herself alongside Victorio, saw her almost succeed, and his heart
thundered wildly as he stared back at those fixed glaring eyes
and foam-flecked nostrils. She came on to within a dozen feet
of the gray stallion's tail, but there she clung, unable to close
in. As though an invisible wire held her, she raced on in third
place, with The Iron Duke and Victorio staving off her challenge—but failing to defeat her.

"The rope!" Delgadito shouted. "Throw me the rope!"

Only then did Ponce realize why the lithe wrangler had
forced Desert Storm to pit her strength and speed against the
two stallions. That she had proved herself their equal he
realized, even with his brain reeling from the shock of the
terrifying experience. Heeding the call, he twisted around,
measured the distance and threw the coiled reata. He saw
Delgadito reach out and snatch the whipping end, then face
forward and set himself for the most dangerous part of all.
If the rope tightened too quickly, Victorio would be flung end
over end. At the speed they were traveling, there was no
question as to what would happen to Ponce.

Riding the streaking filly as only an Apache could have
ridden, Delgadito displayed the matchless skill which had
earned him an unquestioned position among his people as a
great horseman. He shortened his grip on the rope and slowly
exerted a pull. At first there was no noticeable effect on the
speed of the madly racing gray. Then the dark legs began to
shorten their stride, the reaching muzzle dropped from that
level line, and The Iron Duke raced on out of reach of the
slowing stallion. It required another fifty yards to haul Victorio around into a long circle. The rope shortened steadily,
his wicked head was brought tight against Desert Storm's
right shoulder, and the two horses plunged to a stop. With
the rasping noise of the winded animals' breathing loud in the
sudden stillness, Ponce and Delgadito sat looking into each

other's eyes without speaking, their faces gray and drawn with the knowledge of the tragedy so narrowly averted.

After a long time, Delgadito drew an unsteady breath, moved Desert Storm away with the pressure of a hand, and started toward the distant corral. A piercing shout from Ponce jerked him around, and he saw the youth staring with stricken eyes at Desert Storm's right leg.

"She is limping, Delgadito!" Ponce cried hoarsely.

Before the man could move, Ponce was off Victorio and running toward his filly. She snorted in fright and leaped to flee, but after one step, she halted, a long shudder running through her as she stood on three legs. The fourth, the right foreleg, was held off the ground. Only then did Delgadito remember that slight hesitation of hers in the instant before she had begun her move against the two stallions.

Desert Storm had raced over a half mile with an injured foreleg!

17

Out of the Valley

DESERT STORM'S brilliant career was finished!

Ponce knew it before Gil Dreen rose from his examination and pronounced sentence. The big filly's last race had been too much for that right foreleg. That she had overcome the near-fatal accident a year ago had been nothing short of miraculous. That the fractured leg had knit and stood up under the punishment she had given it along her rocket-like rise to fame and fortune had been the rest of that miracle. But it was inevitable that it would collapse sooner or later.

The trainer's words fell like frozen raindrops into the waiting silence. They did not shock Ponce . . . did not surprise him. He had already heard them whispered in the deep shadows of his heart. Now they were merely being echoed.

"It's a tendon. It might be strained . . . or bowed. If it's the latter, we all know what that means—her racing days are finished. If it's strained badly, time alone will tell the story. At best, she'll be out of action for a year."

Ponce did not reply. He choked down the lump in his throat and went on caressing the velvety muzzle pressed against his chest. Words could not help Desert Storm. Words could not restore her leg to its steely, spring-like soundness. That came under the heading of miracles . . . and as David

Forrest had said on another occasion, he'd already had one. It was too much to expect a second. He went on stroking the muzzle, his gaze mirroring the pain in the filly's luminous eyes.

"Finished!"

The word echoed and reechoed in the young Apache's ears like the tolling of a death knell. With the unexpected suddenness of the desert storm for which the filly had been named, calamity had struck and knocked her from the pinnacle to which her matchless courage and speed had carried her. Never to run again . . . never to bring the thousands of spectators to their feet in hysterical uproar . . . never to drink the wind in full flight . . .

It was too much. Ponce put his hands over Desert Storm's eyes, laid his face against the wide forehead and felt hot tears drop from his eyes onto the face of his beloved.

Gabe Stuart climbed down from his roan gelding and went to the boy, who had become like his own flesh and blood in the past four years. "Son," he said gently. There was no answer, no sound at all, and he knew that Ponce was too proud, even in his terrible grief, to reveal the tears that were, to him, unmanly. He said again, "Son," and put an arm across the bowed shoulders.

The silence ran on and on. At long last, Ponce drew an unsteady breath, squared his shoulders and turned. Indianlike, he had gained complete control of his emotions in the space of that one long breath, but his voice was husky and strained.

"What Mr. Dreen tells me to do, I will do."

"Good boy!" Gabe said heartily. "And you won't be doin' it alone. We'll give her the kind of care no horse ever had before." He paused, then said more strongly, "It'll be all right, son! We've got to believe that!"

Delgadito had stood at Victorio's head like a statue of bronze all this while. Only two things betrayed his suffering:

his jaws so tightly clamped the skin showed white over the
bunched muscles and his black eyes that stared straight before
him into space. There was no doubt in his mind but that he
alone was responsible for the ruination of Desert Storm. That
he had forced her to give her all in order to save two human
lives and the life of at least one other horse did not matter
now. She was a ruined animal, and he, Delgadito, was responsible for it.

He went over to Ponce and said in Apache, "The shame of
this thing is mine, brother. I let her run, even after I felt
her hesitate."

Ponce read the misery in the handsome face. He reached
out and grasped Delgadito's upper arms firmly. "Never think
that!" he said sternly. "There are three living now who would
have died had you not done so. There is no cause for shame,
Delgadito. No cause at all."

"Desert Storm will never run again," the man said tone-
lessly. "There is shame in that."

"What happened to her this day would have happened
to her on the morrow, or the next day, or the day before she
was to race. No one can say *when* it would have happened.
Know you that!"

The Old Apache had come up on his pony. Now he spoke
for the first time. "Leave off this beating at the door that has
closed," he commanded. "It is Desert Storm who will say what
is to be in its own season. Now is the time to take from her
the pain."

The quiet authority in the voice broke the spell holding
the group motionless and silent around the big filly. Gil Dreen
moved to his horse, unstrapped the saddlebags from behind
the cantle and began rummaging in them.

"I brought an extra set of stocking rolls for The Duke, in
case he needed them," he said, taking four tight rolls of
muslin from one of the bags. "We'll wrap that leg and get
her over in the shade and see what's to be done then."

The Old Apache said, "Wait here," and turned his pony toward the trees. Minutes later, he returned with the familiar earthen jar in the crook of one arm. He slid off his pony and knelt beside the filly's lifted foreleg. As he removed the lid from the jar, a pungent odor rose into the hot afternoon air. In the act of dipping a hand into it, he turned his head and spoke impatiently to the bystanders.

"Joe Marino is over by the corral. That Iron Duke horse is about run off his legs. Go there, my friends. We will follow later with the filly, my son and I."

In his own sure way, he was ordering them away without actually commanding them. In complete silence, the others mounted and rode toward the corral in the trees—all except Delgadito. He started to lead Victorio out, but with a loud snort, the stallion sank back, pulling against the rope. Twice the Apache pulled, and twice Victorio refused to budge from Desert Storm's side. With a helpless shrug, the man glanced at Ponce.

"He says he is not going, brother."

The Old Apache said more impatiently than before, "Then stay you here with him, Delgadito! But be you silent!"

The wrangler nodded, moved as far away as the lead rope would allow and squatted down in the grass to wait.

As on that unhappy occasion a year ago, The Old Apache now dipped his hands into the evil-smelling ointment, smeared a goodly quantity of it on the injured foreleg and began to massage. While his hands kneaded the tendons and muscles with long, caressing strokes, the deep voice lifted in a wild chant that sounded more like fragments of unknown words than any known tongue. Rising, falling, rising again, it went on and on, to weave its mystic spell over the suffering filly. Little by little the trembling ceased to jerk the sweat-drenched hide, and little by little the pain-slowed breathing steadied. And strangest of all, Desert Storm's head drooped, her eyes closed, and she dozed.

Ponce knew the chant, for he had memorized each foreign syllable and phrase under the guidance of Joto a year ago. Then he had performed the curing rites over the fracture, massaging into it The Old, Old Medicine whose secret formula was known only to a few of the most ancient members of the Apache nation. Of all curatives, it was said, The Old, Old Medicine was the most powerful. No one could assert that this was not true, for no one had seen it fail when administered by the hands of ancients who knew its secret.

For over an hour the chant continued. Then The Old Apache stood up, wiping his hands across his leather-clad thighs. "We will lead her slowly to the trees, my son." he said.

Ponce stepped forward, tugging at Desert Storm's mane. She hesitated, shook her head, then went slowly forward at a halting, limping walk, swinging her head up and down with every step.

Ponce walked backwards, never taking his eyes off that tightly bound foreleg. Each time it touched the ground it was jerked up, like a hand touching a red-hot stove lid. Deeper and deeper into him sank the knowledge that the magnificent Thoroughbred would never recover the full use of it.

Joe Marino had taken The Iron Duke some distance away from the corral when they entered the grove, and was walking the colt back and forth to cool him out. Ponce halted Desert Storm close to the heap of sleeping bags and blankets while Delgadito led Victorio on into the corral.

Supper was prepared and eaten in silence that evening. Later, when everyone lay motionless in blankets and sleeping bags, there was silence, but there was no sleep. Four times during the long, dark hours Ponce heard ·The Old Apache rise and steal into the trees where Desert Storm stood tied. Four times he heard the weird chant tremble along the wind and knew that the ancient warrior was praying to the all powerful God of his people to heal the leg of the great Desert Storm.

Long before dawn, Joto came and touched Ponce on the shoulder. "This day go you with your friends from this place. Go now."

Ponce was out of his blankets and on his feet with one movement of his body. "That is not possible, my father!" he exclaimed in a hoarse whisper. "Desert Storm cannot travel with but three good legs!"

In the chill gloom The Old Apache's face could not be seen. He looked like some gnarled tree-trunk as he crouched under his tattered blanket, and his voice sounded like the far echo of a fading thunder storm.

"Desert Storm goes not from here, my son. With me she will stay. With me she will return, when the time is right." He paused and seemed to be waiting for the young man to protest. When that did not happen, he came closer and laid a bony hand on Ponce's shoulder.

"My son," he said in a lost voice, "help me now to have the faith I have always tried to give you. I have walked down the long trail of life without fear, because one does not fear any thing he sees clearly. Now it is as though I had walked too far—as though I had gone beyond the end of the trail to where the darkness begins. I cannot see clearly. I can but feel my way through this new, unknown darkness, and I must be alone. Somewhere ahead the answer lies waiting. Somewhere there is light. I know that, but I must first pass through the darkness. Go you with Victorio. His feet are almost upon the trail of brightness and glory. You must not hold him back, my son."

Ponce felt the fingers burn into his skin, and wondered with one part of his brain if the heat came from The Old, Old Medicine the hand had been massaging into the filly's leg, or from the fires that still burned in this oldest of Apaches. He said quietly, "It shall be as you say, my father," and started to turn, but another thought pulled him back. "Only tell me what I can believe while I wait."

Joto gripped the youth's shoulders with both hands. "What is the name of your stallion?" he asked sternly.

"Victorio," Ponce replied. "The Victorious One."

"Then believe you this," the ancient warrior commanded in the same firm voice. "War is for the valiant and the brave and the strong—only for them. Shame and death belong to the coward. The spoils of war and the glory of war go always to the victorious one."

Ponce said softly, "I will believe that, my father," and went to wake the others.

An hour later, the five whites and four Apaches rode out of the trees toward the steep trail. On Victorio's head was an Indian bridle, fashioned of a rope that could be decidedly uncomfortable if the stallion acted badly. Dallo Chie and Juan sided him, and Delgadito kept his stocky bay two yards in front of him. The wrangler constantly looked back, watching for telltale signs of danger.

On the level plain outside the valley, Delgadito drew up. "On the way out of these mountains," he cautioned the others, "the path is often steep and dangerous. Go you always carefully, and keep you always safely ahead of Victorio." The next moment, he was leading the way toward the trail that climbed down from this upland plain.

It was mid-afternoon when they left the gloom of the last canyon and emerged into the dancing heat waves of the desert. A short distance away, the big truck and pick-up stood waiting. Delgadito again broke the silence that had lasted throughout most of the trip.

"Dallo Chie, Juan and I will go with Ponce and Victorio. We will be at the place called Shady Mesa at dawn tomorrow. Have you ready for Victorio a strongly built stall."

He nodded to the white people, then turned and led out at a distance-eating canter, along the base of the mountains.

18

The Skies Crash Down

VICTORIO circled his padded stall, paused before the door and screamed a challenge at The Iron Duke across the fifty-foot lot. Then he flung his head in that high, circling movement, reared to paw the steel netting over the opening and dropped to all fours, only to circle the stall again.

This had been going on for a week. It was not only The Iron Duke who served to keep the big gray in constant movement. All the sights and noises and odors of Shady Mesa had a maddening effect on him. Accustomed throughout his life to the clean winds and the endless vistas of his empty mountains, he was like a newly caught lion suddenly flung into a cage and placed on exhibition.

Only the Indian bridle had made it possible for the Apaches to control him upon their arrival at Shady Mesa. Safely locked in the stud box* prepared for him, he had thrown himself about in a frenzy of rage and terror. Within the first four days he lost over a hundred pounds. Now, seven days after his arrival, he looked like an over-trained racer. His bones stuck out like those of a starved animal, and still the oats in the corner

* A stud box is a box stall, heavily reinforced and barred. Often stallions are housed in "stud barns," buildings set apart from the main stables.

183

feed box remained untouched. But, if his flesh was falling away, his anger was not.

Four times the Indian bridle had been put in place and he had been led out, cross-held by Ponce and Delgadito, on the theory he would calm down somewhat if released from the confines of his stall. The outings proved to be a waste of time and energy for all concerned, and after an hour, he had been locked in again, to resume his tireless circling and screaming.

No animal is more easily disturbed than the Thoroughbred racehorse. The slightest change in schedules can throw one into a decline. The slightest fright can bring on a nervous collapse. They will not work properly, if their nerves—consequently their digestive systems—are upset. Victorio's effect on the Forrest racers was becoming serious. Daily, their nervousness had increased, until it had been necessary to turn all except The Iron Duke and Mad Love into distant pastures.

Now, with the stables empty of all save the three male horses, Gil Dreen was unlocking The Iron Duke's door, in preparation for another attempt to solve the problem facing them. Joe Marino was just entering Mad Love's stall. Ponce and his three Apache companions waited in silence before Victorio's stall. The boy felt a wave of pity sweep over him as he watched The Iron Duke come into the open behind Gil Dreen. The colt was frightened and angry, but he stood obediently as the trainer slipped the bridle on, then cinched the training saddle into place. Only his constantly-turning head and backed ears betrayed his rage as he was forced to bear the insulting challenges of Victorio without replying.

Mad Love was by no means the intelligent animal his stable mate was. He flashed out of his stall like a rocket, his blood-bay coat gleaming in the sunlight as he hit the end of the lead shank and whirled. Quite clearly he had no intention of bearing the new arrival's insults with The Iron Duke's dignity. He wanted to fight, and he wanted to fight *now!* It required the combined efforts of David Forrest, Barbara and Joe Marino to subdue him and get him saddled. He was dripping with sweat by the time he passed Victorio's stall on the way to the training track.

Gil Dreen, watching the whole thing, called disgustedly, "Put the blinkers on the crazy fool, Mr. Forrest. We'll work him a little in front of Victorio. If he can't see the gray, maybe he'll calm down."

Mad Love was taken out of sight around the end of the stable while a hood with bulbous leather cups was fetched and slipped onto his head. As he went through the gate, he seemed to be calming down somewhat. The Iron Duke followed.

With the help of his companions, Ponce fitted the scarlet hood over Victorio's head. Delgadito again made the severe Indian bridle, and then Dallo Chie and Juan lifted the saddle, with its hundred pounds of lead weights, and cinched it into place.

Riding the cross-held stallion toward the track, Ponce forced himself to think calmly, to remember the detailed instructions Gil Dreen had given him. He dismissed the little crowd of grooms, stable-hands and exercise boys from his mind as he started through the gate. When Delgadito stepped up and unsnapped the lead shanks, he was thinking only of the business at hand. If this attempt failed . . . He shook his head, and glanced up the track.

The Iron Duke and Mad Love were walking toward him under tight rein. They came on, passing within twenty feet of Victorio. They were going past when, with no gathering of his bulging muscles, Victorio screamed and lunged. Instantly, Ponce jerked hard on the reins, and the burning pressure of the bridle stopped the stallion in his tracks. But it did not end the matter.

The Iron Duke snorted and went wide, fighting to run. Mad Love squealed shrilly and whirled to meet the gray. He was set back on his rump by Joe Marino; but he squealed and

lunged again as the jockey's heavy whip popped against his
shoulder. Unable to grab the bit, he allowed himself to be
turned down the track with The Iron Duke.

Ponce eased his grip on the reins, and Victorio moved forward. He took three steps and shot ahead; but again he stiffened his legs and plowed to a halt as the nerves in his head
jangled under the biting Indian rope. The half-mile track
seemed incredibly long to Ponce during the next hour as it
was circled in a series of soaring leaps and jarring bounds and
skidding stops. His arms and shoulders ached from the strain
of pulling Victorio down, and his head began to throb
steadily.

Following Gil Dreen's directions, he gradually let the stallion come up behind the two racers. By the time they had
circled the track twice, the three horses were less than ten
feet apart. What was more important, they were moving with
some degree of calmness. They went around twice more at a
walk, then the trainer turned and grinned at Ponce.

"Those weights, the bridle and all his foolishness are beginning to make him wonder if he's so big and bad after all,
eh?" he said. "If he gets any more lather on him, he'll look
like he's ready to be shaved."

Ponce never took his eyes off the small, flattened ears.
"He is tiring," he said. "His action is getting rougher all the
time."

Gil Dreen muttered something to his companion, and Joe
Marino turned to inspect the stallion. After a moment, he
pursed his lips and nodded.

"He'll play heck catchin' us," he stated. "Let's let 'em out,
Gil."

"All right," the trainer said to Ponce. "We'll move out a
little. You let Victorio hold his place right where he is on
our tails."

Like perfectly timed machines, The Iron Duke and Mad
Love went into an effortless canter, and Victorio lunged ahead

with the slackening of the reins. All too clearly he intended to run the two racers down; but each time his action shifted, Ponce tightened the reins and he was forced to follow the rose gray and the blood bay at a slow canter.

The starting post neared, dropped behind, and the first turn loomed close. They went around the track once, twice, three times. So gradually as to be almost unnoticeable, the beat of the leaders' hoofs quickened, until they were drumming a steady tattoo on the firm track.

Victorio held his place in the rear.

At the top of the home stretch for the fourth time, Gil Dreen and Joe Marino twisted around to observe the results of the experiment. They stared intently, frowning and exchanging glances. Gil Dreen muttered something under his breath and let The Iron Duke out another notch. The racers' action shifted, smoothing out and quickening as they went into their gliding sprint.

Victorio held his place. His action did not change.

"That stud hasn't picked up his stride by so much as a split second!" Joe Marino yelled unbelievingly. "He just *lengthens* them!"

It was true. Victorio's action did not change, did not quicken. His flaring nostrils were within half a length of The Iron Duke's tail, held there with no apparent effort on his part. Instead of picking up his stride, as the majority of racers do, he lengthened them. They continued steadily, effortlessly and surprisingly long. The big form was settled lower and extended farther. And everyone who watched him realized that he was one of those rare striders* whose speed lies in his ability to stride longer, instead of more quickly.

"When *would* he quicken his action?"

---

* A *strider* is one of that rare species of racers described above. The immortal *Man O' War* was such an animal. At full speed, his strides measured twenty-one feet. The recently retired *Native Dancer*, another all-time-great, has the same action.

The question ran back and forth among the spectators along the rail, and the obvious answer ran with it.

"When he starts to drive."

"All right!" Gil Dreen shouted back into the stallion's face. "Let's just *see* you hold that action of yours now!"

He faced front, bunched himself into a ball over The Iron Duke's shoulders and gave the colt a free rein and the whip. Joe Marino moved with him, and together they sent both racers into a dazzling sprint down the backstretch. Their hoofs rolled deep thunder from the raked and rolled sand as they backed their ears and flattened themselves out and ran their best. Kept in racing form constantly, they were good for a mile at that speed. They went at that mile with the flawless, floating action of truly great runners.

Victorio, still running lazily, stayed with them.

At the three-quarters pole, the riders astride the leaders whipped around. Their eyes almost popped from their heads when they saw Victorio's head swinging with the measured rhythm of a pendulum, less than a half length behind.

"All right! All right!" Gil Dreen yelled hoarsely, "Bring him up here between us, Ponce!"

As the two racers decreased their speed slightly, Ponce held Victorio's head steady, guiding it between the churning hindquarters of the other two. It went up until the crimson hood was on a line with the others. In perfect unison, then, the blood bay, the rose gray and the big dappled gray flashed around the far turn and streaked down the stretch.

At the finish line Gil Dreen yelled, "Take him on, Ponce!" and began to pull The Iron Duke down. Mad Love slowed likewise, as Victorio thundered on into the turn. Midway down the backstretch Ponce began to exert a pull on the reins. Victorio gradually slowed. In the far turn, he was cantering, and at the top of the stretch he was walking down the middle of the track, blowing like a steam engine. When the two racers came up to meet him and swung in on either side, he flattened his ears, but he did not attempt to give battle. All the fight had been run out of him.

"And *that,*" Gil Dreen stated loudly, "is the cure for what ails *him!*"

Every day for two weeks it was repeated. At the end of that time, Gil Dreen put Barbara and Joe Marino up on Last Laugh and a sleek bay named Wild Dreams and sent them to the track. "Victorio has just about run The Duke and Mad Love off their feet," he explained to Ponce with a wry grin. "While they take a breather, we'll let your big boy get used to having girls around."

The first outing in the company of fillies threatened to go much as the first one had gone with the two colts. But after a half dozen attempts to break free, Victorio settled and conducted himself with something remotely resembling dignity. In the closing sprint of the work* Wild Dreams proved unequal to the task of siding the giant gray and the flashy chestnut. She fell off at the top of the stretch and left her fleeter stable mate to fight it out alone.

But the $40,000 sprinter shocked everyone by washing out midway down the stretch. Running furiously, she finished a bad second to the lazily-striding Victorio.

Ten minutes later, the skies crashed down about Ponce.

Walking Victorio on around the track, he looked across the long oval to where the usual cluster of watchers were grouped near the gate. He saw two strangers standing not far from David Forrest. When, a few minutes later, he stopped a short distance from the gate, he recognized one of the new arrivals as the famous sports writer, Ernest Elsner, from Los Angeles. He nodded as Elsner stepped to the rail and waved, then pulled his attention back to Victorio, who was moving restlessly.

For no apparent reason, the gray had become nervous. He

* A *work* differs from exercise or a work-out in that the racer is not permitted to loaf at any time. He is moved exactly as he will be asked to move in a race.

had long since learned the wisdom of avoiding the painful
pressure of the Indian bridle. For the most part, he contented
himself with making dire threats about what he would do if
there were any hope of getting away with it. Now he was
dancing uneasily, backing, half-rearing and trying to swing up
the track. When Ponce jerked him to a standstill, he froze;
but his nostrils were distended, and his ears were flattened
against his head. Ponce did not need to see the eyes to know
that they were once again glazed and blank. Everything about
the tense, quivering animal bespoke stark fear and rage.

Puzzled, Ponce looked up. Something, or someone, was responsible for Victorio's strange behavior. The young Apache
had met the writer at Santa Anita a year ago, and he knew the
man had a way with horses. He could not be the cause. The
second man was a complete stranger. He stood close to Elsner
and, like the writer, was giving Victorio his undivided attention. Heavy, with highly colored features and little eyes set in
deep rolls of fat, he possessed the smallest hands Ponce had
ever seen on a man. The young Apache noticed that David

Forrest was standing quite still, a little distance behind the heavy stranger. He also noticed that his mentor's usually kindly face was unusually pale and stern.

Strangely, no one was talking. The unnatural silence was broken finally by the stranger, who moved along the rail and through the gate. "Bring him over here, boy," he commanded.

Ponce moved Victorio forward, then struck the gray's left shoulder with the whip as the stallion tried to rear. His eyes darkened. This was the first time Victorio had displayed such bad manners in more than a week. He jerked on the reins, and Victorio froze, but he would not budge when Ponce attempted to put him up to the stranger. As the man moved forward, a deep shudder ran through the lathered body. It was then Ponce realized that Victorio knew this man . . . and feared him! He would have taken the stallion away, but the man was close to the quivering shoulder, and one of those small hands was lifting toward the silvery mane. For one awful instant, seeing the hand come up, Ponce was on the verge of letting Victorio do as he wished with the hated and feared stranger.

The fingers parted the coarse hairs. The small eyes stared intently at the marks at the top of the heavy neck. The fleshy face flushed, then paled, and the man turned. He took three steps toward the people at the rail, one arm lifting, one finger pointing squarely at Victorio. His voice, shattering the silence, was like a suffocating hand flung across Ponce's mouth.

"That *wild* stallion is a four-year-old Thoroughbred colt! *And he belongs to me!*"

19

A Filly Named Hagar*

IN THE shocked silence, Gabe Stuart's voice was like a thunder clap.

"That's a lie!"

The people at the rail turned to see the old rancher sitting his roan gelding fifty feet away. He had come up without being noticed, but everyone noticed him now. He was glaring at the heavy stranger like a desert wolf ready to spring. A lane opened for him as he touched spurs to the gelding, went onto the track and halted directly in front of the startled man.

"That stud's name is Victorio, and he was run down and captured in the mountains, a hundred and fifty miles from here. He was as wild as any animal I ever set eyes on." He paused, leaned down and flung his voice into the upturned face. *"An' he belongs to that boy that's settin' on him this minute!"*

The stranger turned to look at Ponce, then jerked back to face Gabe. "You know a little too much, friend!" he snapped. "You'll know a little more when you look at that brand on the left side of that gray's neck. You'll see an ST burned into

---

* An ancient Hebrew word meaning "flight" (pronounced Hay-gar). The story related later in the chapter is true in every respect, but one. The filly's name has been changed.

the hide. And you'll know still more when I tell you my name is Stafford Thomas!"

At mention of the brand, Gabe Stuart jerked upright, all the color draining from his face. He turned startled eyes on Ponce. "That true, son?" he asked hoarsely.

"Yes," Ponce answered quietly. "The brand is there. I have seen it. I should have spoken of it, but I did not because I hoped it was some kind of birthmark, even though I knew it was not."

"Oh, *son!*"

The words sounded as if they had been dragged out of the old man against his will. "You *know* what a brand means! You *know* a branded animal has got to be turned over to the man that branded him! Why did you keep still about it? *Why?*"

Ponce could not reply, could not do anything except move his head from side to side. How did one explain that his silence had been a wild hope he had clutched to his heart throughout the days and nights following his discovery of those two letters? How did one explain that his silence had been the only means of holding onto a dream that must die? How did one explain? He heard his voice and did not recognize it as his own.

"It is over now. Take your horse, Mr. Thomas."

For the second time an unexpected voice cut through the heavy silence.

"Not just yet, I think," said David Forrest.

Unmindful of the eyes turned on him, he stooped and went under the rail and crossed to the man who had introduced himself as Stafford Thomas. He held his shoulders stiffly set, and his eyes glinted with a light Ponce had never seen in them before. Nor had he ever heard the soft-spoken owner use that cold, cutting tone before.

"I will put no more trust in your words than I ever did, Mr. Thomas," he said icily. "This horse will remain in this young man's hands until definite proof is produced to support your claim."

"*Proof?*" Thomas shouted. "My brand is my proof! Every animal in my stable is branded with that ST, and you know it! A little over three years ago, this gray colt broke out of his paddock and was never seen again. He belongs to me, and he's going to my place outside Phoenix as fast as a truck can get him there!"

David Forrest moved a step nearer. "You are on my land, Mr. Thomas," he said, still in that icy tone. "You will leave now, and you will not come back until you have in your hands the registration papers that will prove this colt is yours."

The heavy man choked and coughed in helpless rage. He said in a strangled voice, "You'll not talk so high and mighty when I've done with you, David Forrest! You'll find out what a fool you've been when I come back with the sheriff and the papers stating that this four-year-old was registered as Ishmael, a gray colt with four black stockings, by Equalizer and out of Hagar!"

David Forrest gasped as though Thomas had struck him in the pit of the stomach. "Did you say *Hagar?*" he whispered.

"Yes," Thomas yelled, his eyes shining triumphantly. "I said *Hagar!* You know the mare, I believe?"

"*Get out!*"

David Forrest's voice was the roar of a raging lion. An icy chill shook Ponce as he stared into the owner's ashen face, in which the eyes blazed like living flames. He could not recognize the dignified gentleman he had known for over a year. This tall man was on the verge of destroying the heavy figure before him. In breathless fascination, he watched the two men face each other for a long, tense moment, and he breathed again only when he saw David Forrest control himself with an effort.

"If you are on my land five minutes from now," said the wealthy breeder, "I will kill you with my own hands."

Thomas stared into the cold gray eyes one instant more, then turned and walked rapidly through the gate. He was just beyond the clustered bystanders when Gabe Stuart reined the roan gelding around and jumped it out in front of him.

"I think you and me and a friend of mine will take a little ride, Thomas," Gabe drawled softly. Without taking his eyes from the startled man, he said, "Delgadito, come over here and escort Thomas to his car. Wait for me there."

The lithe Apache moved up without a word and fell in behind Thomas as the man started walking swiftly toward the buildings, fifty yards distant.

Gabe swung down and tossed the gelding's reins to Dallo Chie. "Put him up someplace until I get back," he said and strode off in the wake of Thomas and Delgadito.

No one spoke until a streamer of dust could be seen streaking out across the desert beyond the buildings. Then Ponce moved Victorio over to David Forrest. Out of the corner of his eye, he saw Barbara and Joe Marino come closer. Then, the groom and exercise boys and stable hands closed in to form a loose ring about the silent owner.

"He will return, Mr. Forrest," Ponce said quietly. "It is over now, but I would know about Victorio's mother—the mare called Hagar."

David Forrest shook his head quickly, but he stopped the movement and motioned toward Joe Marino. "He knew her better than I did," he said.

"No," the rider said huskily, "you tell her story, Mr. Forrest. Ponce has got a right to hear it."

The tall man drew a deep breath. "All right," he agreed, "I'll tell it, but it's a story to be kept inside the racing circle. It's ugly—the ugliest in the world—and those like it are few and far between, thank God. They happen now and then—like murders—but they aren't typical of our ways, as I think you'll agree.

"Several years ago, the Irish-bred five-year-old filly named

Hagar was shipped to the United States to race. She had a
nickname—in fact, she had two of them. In Ireland she was
called 'The Rose of Ireland,' but when she arrived in the
States, some joker took one look and named her 'The Gutted
Reindeer.' If you'd seen her, you'd have known why. She
was a strange looking creature, with the longest, most delicate
legs I've ever seen on a Thoroughbred, the finest head and the
biggest belly that ever an aged brood-mare lugged around.
When people saw her in her stall, or being saddled in the
paddock, they laughed at her. She looked bloated, and she
moved stiffly and heavily.

"But when she stepped onto the track for the parade to
the post, she started to burn all over! Her belly was sucked up
until she looked half starved; her head dipped in until her chin
rubbed her chest. And her tail stuck straight up and floated
behind her like a battle pennant in the wind. When she broke
from the starting gate, she did it like a jet fighter. Every time
I watched those fantastically long legs of hers blurring like
dark spokes in a stretch drive, I thought how perfectly the
'Reindeer' part of her nick name suited her. You had to see
her to believe any animal could run as she ran—and even
then you were never quite sure you hadn't been dreaming. She
raced two seasons, and in forty starts she finished first forty
times, going away. She didn't run with fillies and mares; but
with colts and adult troupers, and at the close of her first
season she was carrying top weight in the big handicaps. She
broke three world records and set them again and broke them
again. She was a distance runner. I think her shortest race
was the mile, and she did it as if she were breezing.*

"Her left foreleg gave her a little trouble that first year,
but never enough to cause her owners to scratch** her. The

---

* The term breezing implies letting the horse choose its own speed, as
opposed to driving, which implies pressure exerted by the rider to attain maxi-
mum speed.
** To scratch a horse is to strike his name from the racing card which is
set up by the Race Secretary of the track.

second year she was pulled* six times. That leg was threatening to crack up. She won all the big races back east, however, and then she dropped out of sight as if the ground had opened and swallowed her.

"A couple years later, I found that she'd broken down in the Arlington Special, at Chicago, and had passed from hand to hand until she finally went through the auction ring for $500. I couldn't believe it at first, but later it was verified by the boy who'd ridden her in every one of her forty races.

"Six years went by, and I heard nothing more about Hagar, except that she had produced two colts that were threatening to follow in her footprints. They were both grays and both giants, and they had their dam's rocket-like speed and her endurance. Maybe you've heard of Equalizer and Equity?"

He paused and glanced around at his listeners, who nodded. "They were Hagar's sons by Equipoise," he said quietly.

"Dad!" Barbara cried. "You mean to say Victorio is a brother to those two triple-crown winners?"

"No," David Forrest answered with a slight smile, "you forgot what Mr. Thomas said. Victorio is Ishmael, out of Hagar, by Equalizer."

Ponce was shocked. "You mean they bred Hagar to her own son?" he asked.

"*The best to the best for the best*" the owner quoted. He saw the concern on the young man's face and explained. "We do it once in a while, son. When we have two outstanding examples of a particular blood line, we inbreed to strengthen the line—to preserve the fine points of the dam and the sire. It is never repeated with another relative. An in-breed is always followed by an out-cross, in other words, with an entirely different line. The Iron Duke is a double grandson of City O' Steel and The Dutchess. I wouldn't say he's a bad example of in-breeding. Would you?"

Ponce took a moment to digest this information. At last

* Pull is synonymous with scratch.

he shook his head. "No, I would not say that. And now, will you continue Hagar's story, Mr. Forrest?"

"Now," the man continued, "the story gets ugly. Hagar's owner pulled her out of retirement and put her back into training."

"No!" exclaimed Gil Dreen in a shocked tone. "Why, she was a five-year-old when she came over from Ireland! She was a seven-year-old when she went through the auction ring. If she produced three foals, she'd have been eleven years old, at least! No decent man would try to bring her back at that age—not with her legs gone bad!"

David Forrest nodded slowly. "You're right, Gil. No decent man would. But Stafford Thomas did."

This time it was Barbara who broke in. "You mean that man who was just here, Dad? Did *he* own Hagar?"

Again David Forrest nodded. "He owned her, all right. And, Gil, she wasn't an eleven-year-old. She was twelve—almost thirteen." He saw disbelief change the trainer's face, and added emphatically, "I know it's true, because I heard this part of the whole criminal story from Will Willard, who was Thomas' trainer at the time. You know Will as well as I do, and you know he doesn't make things up. He quit when he got orders to put Hagar back into training. I ran across him about a month after he left Thomas, and the minute I learned what that fiend was planning to do with Hagar I went to him and offered to buy her at whatever price he would name. He turned me down cold. I went up to $50,000—more than I could afford at the time. It was no deal. Do you know why? Impossible as it seems, Thomas had just found out who Hagar was! With her papers and family tree right under his nose, he never connected the broken-down broodmare in his stable with 'The Gutted Reindeer.' When he did, he set out to prove it for himself. You can pretty well see what kind of a horseman Thomas is by that.

"*He knew she couldn't come back!*" David Forrest shouted,

as if to convince himself the thing had not happened. "He knew it, but he made her do it anyway!

"I won't dwell on the details. Hagar, as a thirteen-year-old who had produced three big foals, wasn't the 'Reindeer' she'd been seven years earlier. Game as she was—and that mare gave a new meaning to that word, I tell you—she couldn't come back. Her wind was gone, and her legs were gone—both forelegs. They raced her with inhumanely tight stockings, and those stockings hurt her, as you can well imagine. But she couldn't run without them.

"She raced one season in classes that made a man sick. She followed the county and state fair circuit and at first she ran in the money, such as it was—you know—$200 and $400 purses. Her legs got worse and worse. Finally, she was barred from every track in the United States. That should have stopped Thomas. But it didn't.

"He took her to Mexico!

"She ran just twice at Caliente. I saw her second race . . . and her last. I'll never forget it as long as I live. Sometimes I dream it all over again and wake up in a cold sweat, wanting to kill the man responsible for what happened to that glorious, broken, magnificent Hagar!"

His voice broke, and he could not go on for a moment. His hands were shaking, and he clenched them into fists at his sides. After a while he continued unsteadily, "I don't like to talk about it. It makes me sick even to think about it."

Ponce crossed his hands on Victorio's neck and realized they were icy and damp. For an instant he glimpsed Joe Marino's face, and when he saw the expression of agony on it, a feeling of mystery and of suspense began to beat its way into his brain. He said very softly, "We would hear about Hagar, Mr. Forrest, if you can tell us."

The tall man looked up, his eyes meeting Ponce's. He drew a long breath, like a diver preparing for the plunge, and locked his hands together in front of him.

"It was in the sixth race at Caliente, and it was on one of
those still days, with the thermometer standing over 115 de-
grees. I had gone to the barns that morning to again try to buy
Hagar from Thomas. Again I told him to name his own
figure, but it was no use. I tell you, it was as if that man hated
Hagar for breaking down and was determined to *make* her
do something she *couldn't* do any more. I saw her standing in
her stall with her bones sticking out like sharp sticks under
her carelessly-groomed coat, and I bawled like a baby. She was
almost white by then, with just her mane and tail still dark.
She was a sick mare. Any kid could have seen that. But she was
entered in the sixth race, and she was going to run, if it
killed her.

"She went to the post with her front legs wrapped so
tightly she could hardly move, but when her rider started
warming her up, she seemed to come to life again. Broken as
she was, she couldn't help stepping out when the call to post
went through her.

"She broke slow. In fact, she was ten lengths behind the
last horse going into the first turn. It was a mile race—an impossible distance for her at her age, even if she'd been in top
condition—but a hundred feet from the turn she started to
move.

"I don't know where she found the strength, nor the wind,
for that sprint, but she moved up on the field, and halfway
around the turn she caught the leaders. She began pulling
away from them. It was impossible, I tell you! Impossible! But
she did it.

"For one instant, coming down the home lane, she ran as
she had run seven years before, her fine head pointed straight
out, her long body flattened—and those incredibly long legs—
those reindeer legs—those ruined legs—flashed like the spokes
of a rolling wheel.

"One instant only, a hundred yards from the wire, she
screamed—just once. I knew what had happened, and I knew

she was going to fall, but she didn't! With the leaders closing up on her, she held them off—and she started stumbling. She looked as if she were running downhill—falling with every stride.

"She went under the wire three lengths ahead of the leaders. And then, when her rider started to ease her in, she went down, as if a wire had tripped her. In full stride, she collapsed and hit the dirt and skidded fifty feet. When she tried to get up, both front legs buckled under her like wet rags. I knew then that I had been right when I saw her stumble at the head of the stretch.

"She had run over a hundred yards with both forelegs broken!"

There was a loud gasp from the tense listeners, and Barbara's great sob rose into the morning air like the cry of a wounded creature. There were tears in the eyes of David Forrest, and when Ponce glanced at Joe Marino, he was shocked to see tears streaming down the rider's quivering cheeks. Gil Dreen had bent his head and was whispering to himself in a steady, furious monotone, his usually calm face pale and drawn.

Ponce looked down into David Forrest's wet eyes. "Finish it, Mr. Forrest," he whispered. "What did Hagar's owner do?"

"Nothing," said the other hoarsely. "He didn't even come onto the track to look at her. But I did. I stood there, and for one sickening moment I watched her try to get those shattered legs of hers under her. She floundered in the dust like a bird with broken wings. Her rider grabbed her head and tried to keep her from hurting herself. He was just a kid, and he was crying as if his heart were broken. I can still hear him whispering, 'Hagar! Oh, Hagar! Don't try to get up, honey! Die quickly, sweetheart . . . so they can't hurt you any more!' "

"I told the vet to put her to sleep as fast as he could. When she lay back, her big eyes were fixed on her rider's face. He took her head in his arms and sat there crying over her while she died. Even when they hitched a team to her hind legs and dragged her away, that boy followed along behind, holding that beautiful head off the ground.

"I had a grave made, and we buried Hagar that evening— just her rider and I. Three days later, I went back to the grave with a little headstone I had had carved, but there was already a headstone there. I knew Hagar's rider had put it there. A big blanket of roses covered the grave—and I knew that boy had probably spent his last cent on those flowers. The wording on the marble gravestone said:

> HAGAR, THE ROSE OF IRELAND
> FAIREST OF THE FAIR
> AND WINNER TO THE END"

Ponce could not see for the tears blinding him, but he could still picture Joe Marino's white, quivering face, and he could hear Barbara weeping wildly in her father's arms. He turned, wanting to escape to the silence of the distant desert, but David Forrest's voice held him motionless.

"When I read those words, I went and found the rider. I asked him if he would come to my stables and ride for me. I didn't even know his name until he wrote it on the contract I gave him."

Barbara looked up through streaming eyes. "Who was he, Dad?"

The tall horseman smiled faintly. "You know him, honey. He's right behind you. His name is Joe Marino."

20

The World Goes Crazy

BECAUSE she had perched herself atop the high wall that enclosed the spacious patio on three sides, Barbara was the first to see the streamer of dust in the distance. She could not be certain, at first, because the lowering sun was in her eyes. She squinted and put both hands up to shade her eyes. No, she had not been mistaken. It was dust, and it was being raised by a speeding car. She shouted, "Here they come!" and turned to clamber off the eight-foot-high wall.

Joe Marino and Ponce jumped forward to catch her ankles and lower her, but she released her hold before they were prepared. In a tangle of arms, legs and bodies, the three young people landed on the ground, grunting with surprise.

Alice Forrest tried to instruct her tom-boyish daughter in lady-like conduct without apparent success, because she could not keep her face straight.

"Barbara!" she said in what was meant to be a stern voice. "Young ladies do not climb walls, and if they *do*, they don't jump off them and knock everyone silly! Get up off the ground and straighten yourself out."

The "young lady" did not appear particularly downcast. She was glowering at Joe Marino, who still lay across her feet, trying to get his breath. "Stop acting as if you were dying!"

she ordered. "*I'm* the one on the bottom! If you don't get up, they'll be here!"

The Italian jockey groaned much louder than any seriously damaged soul could have groaned and rolled over on his back. "This is it," he whispered in what was meant to sound like his last breath. "I've had it! Think kindly of me . . ."

Barbara tried to wriggle her feet free. "I'll think a lot kindlier of you, if you'll remember your manners and help a lady to her feet," she informed him. "Why didn't you two characters tell me you were going to grab hold of my ankles?"

Ponce rolled and pushed himself erect. "Why didn't you tell us you weighed a ton?" he complained, reaching a hand down to help Barbara up. "Next time . . ." His voice ended in a loud grunt as she seized the extended arm and jerked him down on top of Joe Marino.

"Never mind helping me," the girl grumbled, not bothering to glance at her two fallen companions. "I'll manage on my own—*Oh, there they are!*"

This last was uttered in a completely unladylike yell as she leaped up and dashed out through the wide arch. An instant later, she exclaimed, "Why, *that* isn't Gabe!"

It wasn't Gabe. It was an utter stranger who wheeled the long Cadillac convertible up the drive and brought it to a skidding stop before the archway. It was someone remotely resembling the elderly rancher insofar as facial features were concerned, but this man was dressed in the smartest of smartly tailored English riding togs. When he opened the door and stepped out, his high cordovan boots gleamed in the glow of the sinking sun, and the widely flared breeches showed not a wrinkle nor crease. The strongly cut features were burned to a deep bronze, the blue eyes shone brightly under white brows, and a carefully clipped white moustache edged the upper lip.

David Forrest, coming up behind the gaping Barbara, halted abruptly and did some gaping of his own. He choked and coughed and seemed to be in danger of strangling then and there. He blinked rapidly, his gray eyes beginning to twinkle. Then he stepped forward and extended his hand.

"Welcome to Shady Mesa, stranger," he said gravely. "I'm David Forrest. May I ask your name, please?"

Delgadito spoke from his rigidly upright position on the back seat of the gleaming yellow convertible. "He won't tell," he informed the staring group. "All the way from Phoenix I keep asking, 'Who are you?' and all the time he just keep saying, 'Shut up, smart guy!' "

The red-haired Alice Davis came up and stood close to her husband. Like everyone else, she was staring intently at the new arrival, and like everyone else's, her blue eyes were twinkling merrily. "He's evidently a criminal," she announced matter-of-factly. "You can tell that by watching his eyes. They're shifty. And why else would he refuse to tell whom he is?"

"I don't think so," Gil Dreen disagreed solemnly. "He's a movie star, and he doesn't want anyone to recognize him. That's why he's dressed like a movie star. I've seen him in some of those cheap western pictures. Now who . . ."

It was Ponce who proved unequal to the prolonged strain of play-acting. He stepped close and peered up into the flushed face. "What happened to you, Mr. Gabe?" he inquired seriously. "Who dressed you like this?"

"I dressed me up like this!"

The bull-like roar sent everyone a foot into the air, effectively closing the play. "Is there any law against a man buying some new duds for a change? *Is there?* And since when is it a crime to buy a little old car, I'd like to know? If Gil Dreen can drive a Lincoln, I reckon I can match him any old day in the week!"

No one said anything. The silent scrutiny went on and on, with everyone holding a hand over his or her mouth to hold back the laughter.

"Well?" Gabe demanded loudly, "if everybody's tongue-tied, maybe this will loosen you up!"

He reached into a breast pocket of his tweed jacket and pulled forth a long, creased paper. "Run your eyes over *that*, Mr. Ponce Stuart!" he ordered and leaned back against the Cadillac seat.

Ponce took the paper, unfolded it and started to read. The next instant, he leaped into the air, turned completely around and came down running. He bounded up the curving drive, making for the stables, his voice lifted in a nerve-shattering Apache war cry.

Barbara began, "What—" and bent to retrieve the fluttering paper from the ground. She took one glance, threw the paper into the air and took off in Ponce's wake, doing her best to reproduce the war cry in English.

Everyone stared after the two racing figures, shocked into silence. "My turn," said David Forrest and stepped over to the fallen paper. He straightened. "Sold" he read slowly, "one gray, four-year-old Thoroughbred colt." Then he jumped and almost dropped the paper as Joe Marino's ear-splitting "*Yiiii-yiiii!*" exploded in his ears. The next instant, everyone was staring after the jockey, who was streaking after Ponce and Barbara.

"All right!" the horseman ordered sternly. "Everyone get a good grip on his legs, so they can't move. It says here that Ishmael, otherwise known as Victorio, is the property of one Ponce Stuart. It says . . ." His voice trailed into silence and he was forced to watch his wife, Gil Dreen and Delgadito disobey his order without so much as a "By your leave, sir!" A moment later, he was left alone with Gabe Stuart.

"All right, Gabe," he said quietly. "Let's have it. Just how did you manage this?"

The ex-sheep herder's eyes were twinkling in his bronze face. "It wasn't too hard," he stated casually. "That Thomas feller can be right reasonable, if you handle him right." He

paused, lifting his right hand lazily, and David Forrest saw the dark bruises on the big knuckles. "And I seemed to handle him just right."

David Forrest could not have kept from showing his delight, if his life had depended on keeping his face straight. "Did he put up much of a scrap, Gabe?"

"No scrap at all," the other returned quietly. "About the time he got his mouth open, I bashed him one. He did some thinkin' and came up with just the right answer."

"Aha!" The owner of Shady Mesa made a concentrated

effort to keep his joy in the background. Suddenly his face sobered, and his eyes looked directly into Gabe's. "What did it cost you, Gabe?" he asked quietly. "In money, I mean."

"$10,000," the older man replied.

"You don't have that kind of money."

"I didn't, maybe. I do now."

A suspicious light glimmered in the tall man's gray eyes. "Your cattle?" he murmured.

"All right!" Gabe said loudly. "So I sold 'em! But before you go rakin' me over the coals, let me tell you the honest to gosh truth. All my life I've scraped and raked, tryin' to get enough money to quit the sheep business an' get into the cattle game. I can't explain it, but I *know* I'd never have gotten my cattle if it hadn't been for that there boy Ponce! He's been more than a son to me. You know that. Look what he done this last spring! Pulled Desert Storm out of pasture when the drought struck—pulled her out when the vets said she ought'n to race for another couple months—just to win enough money to put in that there irrigation system! Know anybody else who'd have done a thing like that? I don't! So along comes this Victorio and turns out to be a hot-blood, with more speed than any animal ever could use up in ten lifetimes. You think I was going to set back and see him lose that horse to a skunk like Thomas? Would *you?*"

David Forrest started to shake his head. "I don't know—" he began, then suddenly changed his tone. "No, I think I'd have done just as you did, Gabe."

"Sure you would!" said the other heartily. "So I went to my banker an' told him to get ahold of some riders an' have 'em round up every last critter on my place. I'll get top price for the herd, an' I'll have a nice, tidy sum left over, even after that $10,000 is subtracted. So I did it for my boy Ponce—an' for myself. I found out I don't hanker to look after no cow critters, after all. I got a yen to go into the horse business with

Ponce, an', as of now, you're lookin' right square at Gabe Stuart, horse-trainer-to-be. Look back here."

He half turned and indicated the back seat, which was piled high with books of all sizes and colors.

"What are they?" David Forrest asked, puzzled.

"Horse books!" exclaimed Gabe. "When I get done memorizin' every last one of them, I'll be a trainer beside of which Gil Dreen will look like a mere exercise boy!"

For a long minute David Forrest looked into the bright blue eyes. "I want you to know," he said quietly, "I've been mistaken about you all this time. I always knew you were a good man. You aren't. You're a great man, Mr. Gabe Stuart." He reached out and wrung the rancher's work-calloused hand. "Come along," he invited. "I think we ought to have another look at your first pupil. You'll have your hands full, getting him ready for Santa Anita, you know."

Exactly one week later, a sleek car and trailer rolled through the sleeping town of Arcadia, California, turned onto Huntington Drive, farther on, then right onto Baldwin Avenue, and finally drew up in front of the Receiving Barn at the Santa Anita racing plant. In the front seat sat a distinguished-looking gentleman, obviously a horseman, and a slight youth, obviously an Indian, and just as obviously a rider. On the back seat, bolt upright, sat a third man, with bronze skin and wide-set black eyes in a handsome face.

Delgadito said in a hoarse stage-whisper, "This is Santa Anita, brother?"

Ponce nodded and looked out through the open window at the acres upon acres of long, low barns and towering stands. "Yes," he answered in Apache, "we are here at last, Delgadito. Do your eyes behold beauty?"

"They behold much," the wrangler stated, showing his dazzling teeth in one of his rare smiles. "They have not yet sorted out the beautiful from the ugly, I think."

Gabe Stuart was not thinking about beauty nor ugliness. At the moment, he was concentrating on Gil Dreen's last-minute instructions. "I go in there," he said, as if repeating a well-learned lesson. "I show Victorio's papers to the Race Secretary and ask for the end stall in barn 99. Then I pay them. Got it!"

He opened the door, climbed out and entered the Receiving Barn. When he reappeared an hour later, his face wore a satisfied grin. In a moment, he was guiding the big car down the rows of stalls toward the most distant barn. "Keep your eyes peeled and tell me when to turn," he instructed his companions. "There's sixty-eight . . . seventy-eight . . . ninety-eight . . . guess we turn here . . . nothing ahead . . . Is that ninety-nine up there, son?"

"Yes," Ponce replied. "And there is the last stall. Put on the brakes, Mr. Gabe! That's a fence ahead, not a barn!"

"Okay! Okay!" Gabe said. "Only I don't want to throw Victorio through the front of his trailer into Delgadito's lap! Aha!" He brought the car to a halt with the air of one accomplishing a major undertaking. "We're here!"

That evening, newspapers throughout the country carried the following syndicated column:

OWNER OF LAST YEAR'S HANDICAP WINNER ARRIVES AT SANTA ANITA WITH NEW DARK HORSE

Apache Jockey
On War Trail Again

by Ernest Elsner

Arcadia, Calif. Oct. 3—Who is Victorio? Give up? Then we will tell you: Victorio is a huge, darkly-dappled, gray four-year-old son of Hagar and Equalizer. The Stud Book lists him under the name of Ishmael, but he's Victorio now. In case anyone is inclined to brush the above information aside with an indifferent, 'So what?' let us remind one and all that the word Victorio, when translated, means *The Victorious One*.

And if that hits a dead nerve, let us further inform said scoffers that said colt was so named by his young owner and rider, one Ponce who last year found it not too difficult to boot the fleet Desert Storm—also named by him—under the wire lengths ahead of the odds-on favorite, The Iron Duke. Remember now? Scared yet?

It is by no means our intention to climb out on the proverbial limb to hurl dire predictions of upsets in the offing. We are restricting ourselves to bare facts, believe it or not. The facts are that the aforementioned Ponce acquired the burly gray son of the immortal Hagar by a fluke no one would believe, even if it were told under oath. We are not on the witness stand, so we are not going to impart those details and get ourselves called "Liar!" Suffice it to say that Victorio is here in our midst as of this morning. He can be viewed at your leisure, if you see fit to mosey trackward, 'most any day.

Via the grapevine, we learn that the Black Blitz—otherwise known as Desert Storm—will not be back for the coming season. She may be retired permanently, if the recently-sustained injury to her right foreleg proves incurable, as is feared. It is rumored the injury occurred during a race with the Victorio we mentioned a moment ago. It is likewise rumored that said race was close—mighty close.

Desert Storm, we salute you! Come back, if you can!

To name but a handful of the big names reportedly coming in soon: Trafalgar, the speedy English colt who's been showing a clean set of heels to everything thrown at him in the U.S. is coming out west to show us how it's done out east. Don't Bother Me, the powerhouse that made his rich owner richer last year, is coming out of his year's lay-off, bigger and better than ever, they say. Then there's Blazing High, who's been down South America way recently. He's coming in for the big stakes events. The redoubtable Blue Nose will be down from Canada. And the flashy Stumbler is leaving his native Texas with his usual storehouse full of "Whoppers."

A final word of caution: Don't do anything rash, such as trying to pick a winner! Only one thing is certain, my friends. The world is going crazy—the horse world, that is.

21

Before the Dawn

FOR four days Ponce and Delgadito took turns leading Victorio up and down the rows of barns, around the grounds and onto the training track. More often than not, they found themselves swung off the ground as the stallion reared and threw his head back and forth in an attempt to see everything at once. Gabe was convinced that the sooner Victorio found himself surrounded by the atmosphere he would know for the rest of his life, the better. Victorio, on the other hand, was convinced he was in danger of being murdered in his tracks. He let it be known in no uncertain terms that he disagreed emphatically with his new trainer's views on how a wild stallion should conduct himself.

When in the confines of the roomy stall, the massive gray whiled away the hours by pacing around and around and trying to pick quarrels with various other Thoroughbreds stabled in distant barns. By the end of the fifth day, however, his three handlers began to hold forth some faint hope for his eventual surrender to hard and fast facts. In his stall that night, he frequently paused for minutes at a time to look through the heavy netting. His shrieks abated toward morning. When he was taken to the training track for his first workout under saddle the next morning, he moved restlessly, but without real violence. Everyone began to breathe more easily again—including a vast number of Thoroughbreds, owners, trainers, grooms, stable-hands and riders. The unknown gray had been rapidly becoming the most unpopular resident of Santa Anita.

After that, the young Apache and the gigantic Thoroughbred could be found at the training track, or near it, from 5:30 A.M. until 5:30 P.M., day in and day out. Victorio was placed on a training schedule that would have killed off his more refined cousins within a month. He became a tireless machine, instead of a sensitive, high-strung "hot house" racer. The years spent running the ridges and high plains of the Mogollons had fitted him admirably to meet the fantastic demands made upon his constitution now. Unlike others of his blood, he had escaped the early rigors imposed on young hopefuls. Now, at the peak of his power, he was being readied for a belated entrance into the world he claimed as his own by right of birth. Full grown, hard as iron, swift as an antelope, he was contrary as a mule.

Ponce never mounted him without the heavy quirt and sharp spurs—not in those first weeks. In order to use the rowels to best advantage, it was necessary for him to ride with lengthened stirrups. Other riders, passing on their smooth-as-silk racers, repeatedly turned to stare at the long-haired, dark-skinned jockey who rode with those abnormally long stirrups. They noted also those big rowels and the heavy quirt. They made inquiries in vain, and eventually sought the answers with the proper person—Ponce. They would, one by one, come alongside, slow down and make idle talk for a while. Then it would start.

"Who's the big gray boy?"

"Victorio," Ponce would reply, never taking his eyes off the flattened ears.

"Fast?"

"Maybe."

"Mean?"

"Sometimes." Answering that question, Ponce always asked himself, "Why don't they look at those ears and those eyes?"

There was usually a long pause as the two horses continued their tireless jogging or cantering. Then:

"You always ride with stirrups that long?"

"No."

"How come you're doing it now?"

"So the spurs will catch him where it stings."

"You always carry that whip?"

"No."

"How come you're carrying it now?"

"Sometimes I use it."

"Mean, hunh?"

The wide-set black eyes would come around to the curious one's face, and the hint of a smile would alter the line of the full lips.

"Me—or Victorio?" Ponce would ask.

"Oh! The colt, naturally!"

The black eyes would crinkle at the corners, and Ponce's teeth would gleam in that slow smile of his.

"When Victorio is mean," he would state, "I am mean also."

And later, over coffee and doughnuts in the cafeteria, one of those riders would say to someone else in a low tone, "Y'know . . . that Indian kid is a character! Who the heck is he, anyhow?"

Invariably someone would state, "That's Ponce. Remember last year's Handicap here? He won it goin' away on that black filly of his, Desert Storm. Won half a dozen other classics back east, too."

Gradually the word got around, and everyone took to watching Ponce and Victorio as they kept to their endless circling of the track. With no effort on their part, they were becoming the most talked-about figures at the plant.

Slowly, but surely, the barriers surrounding the professional riders were taken down to admit Ponce to the select ranks. More and more often, he was invited to join the others during meals in the cafeteria. His quiet manner and soft voice provided no excuse for anyone's taking offense at anything he did or said. Whenever he spoke—which was seldom indeed—his new friends listened attentively. When he listened, he did it in a way that left no doubt that he was genuinely interested in everything said. Before long, it became an accepted custom for these horsemen to gather before Victorio's stall in the evenings and talk of the one thing such people discuss, when two or more are assembled—horses.

October was pounded to death by Victorio's racing hoofs. November came and began to swing to the rear. There were long stretches now when Victorio conducted himself for all the world like a well-mannered Thoroughbred. Once in a while, he seemed to recall that he was, after all, an unwilling newcomer to this noisy party. When that happened, the spurs and the whip would help him to change his mind in short order. With a snort and a toss of his big head, he would again take up the briefly-dropped threads and go on weaving the pattern that had no end.

Then November 20th came—and *Trafalgar!*

It was an unusually brilliant morning. The sun drew great clouds of steam from the damp roofs of the barns and the towering stands, until all the world looked as if it were on fire. Riding with shortened stirrups for the first time in many weeks, Ponce held Victorio to a walk until he could become accustomed to his action in this new position. He had been on the track for over an hour and was setting himself more firmly over the gray shoulders, preparing to let Victorio out another notch, when he glanced up and saw the big brown plunge onto the track. It took no second glance to tell him the identity of that rawboned colt. Nor did he have to look twice to know that Trafalgar was giving his rider a difficult time.

Holding Victorio to a measured canter, he came on around. Fifty yards from the new arrival, he heard the rider talking sharply, angrily, and instantly recognized Bob Willis' voice. Eager to greet the blue-eyed rider whom he had beat out in The Arlington Special a few months ago, Ponce moved Victorio ahead more quickly. As they drew even with the brown, he was aware that Victorio's action had changed from a smooth glide to a rough, tense motion. But he held him steady and lifted a hand, calling, "It is good to see you again, Bob Willis!"

Bob Willis did not smile in return, nor even glance around. He was giving all his attention to the rough-going Trafalgar between his knees. His startlingly blue eyes were narrowed, and his thin cheeks were flushed with anger. He said, "Cut it out, you scarecrow, or I'll brain you!" and slammed his bat hard against the colt's right shoulder. Before Victorio could move, he was pinned against the rail.

For days thereafter, those who witnessed the battle tried in vain to discover what actually happened out there on the track. Only Ponce and Bob Willis knew that Trafalgar whirled and struck Victorio in the belly with both hind feet and lifted him a foot off the ground. Only Ponce knew what would happen next—and he was helpless to prevent it.

With the crimson hood shutting Trafalgar from sight, Victorio had made no move to attack when the two of them had been going side by side. He could not see Trafalgar coming at him and so could not avoid being slammed into the rail. He *could* fight back, once his feet came back onto the ground. And he did!

He reared and lunged for the brown's shoulder, and his long yellow teeth clicked like the jaws of a steel trap . . . on

thin air. Trafalgar whirled and lashed out again with both hind feet, but Victorio, anticipating that move, was not there. He had sat down abruptly and swung his front quarters to one side. Then, with a convulsive heave, he lunged in, again trying for that shoulder. Terrified now, Trafalgar tried to escape by whirling around short and dodging up the track. As he jumped, Bob Willis lost a stirrup, clung on for one awful moment, then flew through the air and landed with a terrific impact, fifteen feet away. He did not move as the raging colts wheeled and darted above him, but lay on his face, his hands locked over the back of his head.

Dimly, Ponce was aware of the milling, shouting crowd closing in around the two colts. Dimly, he heard Delgadito shouting to him to use the spurs and the whip. In a flash, he kicked both feet free of the high irons and brought them down in a scissors-like drive against the dappled gray hide. The quirt whispered once as it came down and caught Victorio across his sensitive nostril. And with a shriek of helpless fury,

Victorio shot down the track at a dead run, all the fight knocked out of him.

In the backstretch, Ponce glanced over and saw Trafalgar being led from the track. He breathed deeply when he saw Bob Willis rise to his feet and beat the dust from his faded levis. The young Apache kept Victorio to a run for another mile and a half, then slowed him, when the flattened ears lifted slightly. When at last he pulled the stallion in to a cooling jog, there was a great warmth pulsing through the young man. He had this day learned something that made all the agonies and uncertainties of the last few months worthwhile.

Victorio would not fight unless attacked!

After that, it was a matter of keeping him too busy to think of anything except running. Day after day, he was allowed to breeze for well over a mile. Day after day, he was led out, full of impatience, in the early morning and brought in at 11:30, tired and docile. Some time between November 20 and December 19, Victorio became tame. And one morning Ponce looked into the wide-set, dark eyes and saw that they were as clear as the waters of that lake high in the Mogollons. He did not become excited, did not call Delgadito's and Gabe's attention to his discovery. Almost, he felt humble in the face of the great thing that had come at last into his hands.

Victorio had been deep in his heart for a long time.

Ponce said to Gabe, "It will not be needful to take him to the track this day, Mr. Gabe. Shall we not let him rest?"

Long ago, Gabe Stuart had discovered the wisdom possessed by his adopted son. If Ponce recommended a rest for the gray, a rest was obviously what the gray needed. He nodded. "Whatever you think, son. He looks good enough right now to win the Maturity. I reckon a day off won't hurt him any."

On December 19, Ponce did not bring Victorio in from the track until shortly before sundown. As he rode along in front of Barn 99, he noticed that the place was completely deserted.

Strange, that. Delgadito had never failed to be on hand to help with Victorio. He dismounted and peered into the dim stall. Delgadito might be asleep there—he often was. Empty! Well, then, he would unsaddle Victorio and groom him alone.

As Ponce turned to unstrap the cinch, he spoke sharply. "Stand still, old goat! You try jumping around like that and I will show you who's boss!" He reached up and hauled the high head down. "Be you quiet!"

The big racer was acting strangely. He kept blowing loudly through his nostrils and dancing up and down on his front feet, as if preparing to take a high jump. Suddenly, he lunged away from Ponce, jumped past him and jammed his nose hard against the crack dividing the upper and lower doors of the stall adjoining his. When a loud whinney came from the interior, he reared and brought both forefeet crashing down against the stout boards.

"Victorio!" Ponce shouted sternly, leaping forward to drag the gray away. "Just because that empty stall is no longer empty is no reason for you to act crazy." He lifted a hand and struck the thick neck an open-palm blow. "*Get back!*" he ordered harshly. Suddenly angry, he grabbed the lead rope tied to the ring on the nearby post and snapped the catch in Victorio's bridle ring.

As he went about washing the gray down with a mild solution of liniment water and massaging the long, dark legs, he kept glancing around, expecting to see Gabe or Delgadito returning. They had never failed to be here! By the time he had completed readying Victorio for the night, he was definitely worried. Something had happened—something bad!

He put Victorio into the stall, snapped the lock on the door and turned away. In mid-stride he halted, his glance falling to the half-opened newspaper beside the door. With an impatient frown, he bent and picked it up and started toward the cafeteria. An empty trash-can stood at the corner of Barn 88, and he started to twist the newspaper, preparatory to throwing it into the container. Quite by accident, he glanced at it. Quite by accident, he found himself reading:

FAMED DESERT STORM
TO STAGE COMEBACK IN
HANDICAP!

For one endless moment he stared aghast at the big black letters smeared across the top of the sports section. Then, with hands that shook, he smoothed the paper out and began to read swiftly.

Black Blitz Barges Back
With a Bang!

by Ernest Elsner

Arcadia, Calif. Dec. 19—We should have known better than to be taken in by that conjurer, Ponce! Him and his *dark horses!* Just this day we learned that the renowned Desert Storm is snugly tucked away in Barn 99, at the Santa Anita track. It seems the powerful classics winner from Arizona did not have a bowed tendon, after all—just a strained muscle in her right foreleg. True enough, she is reportedly wearing stockings on both forelegs, but they say the classy gal does it out of sheer vanity—not because she needs them. However that may be, she has been officially nominated to start in The Santa Anita Handicap, come February 25. Needless to say, her appearance on the scene as a contender for the second time in the big 'Cap knocks a good many speculations as to possible winners right into a cocked hat! Breathes there a man with memory so short he does not recall what that black tornado did last year? I think not. I think we will here and now . . ."

Ponce did not finish reading the article. Nor did he deposit the paper in the trash can. He whirled, started to run—and fell flat on his face. He was shouting like a madman as he scrambled up and streaked toward Barn 99 and the closed stall adjoining Victorio's. His fingers were all thumbs as he tore at the latch. Finally it clicked . . . the upper door crashed open . . . and he was gazing straight up into Desert Storm's startled eyes.

The next instant he was inside, pulling the velvety muzzle down against his chest. He did not then remember that tears were for children. Quite unashamedly, he wept. Very unsteadily, he said over and over, "Ah, Desert Storm! You have come back! You have come back!"

22

To the Victor

JANUARY 28, the day of the running of the Santa Anita Maturity, dawned cold and gray. Toward noon, the skies cleared, the sun came out, and the air grew close and warm.

Victorio was taken out early in the morning for a leisurely stroll up and down the cleared area in front of his stall. By eight o'clock, he was back in his stall. With that inborn sensitivity peculiar to Thoroughbreds, he realized that this day was wholly unlike any day he had ever known. Throughout the morning, he circled his stall restlessly, pausing often to look out through the wire netting. One o'clock came, then two o'clock. Then suddenly it was 4:30, and the call to post rang out above the heavy drone of the packed stands.

As nine racers left the chute separating the grandstands from the clubhouse stand and filed onto the track, a waiting hush fell over the grounds, to be broken at length by the announcer clearing his throat into the microphone.

"Ladies and Gentlemen," he said suddenly. "The horses are coming onto the track to begin the parade to the post, in preparation for the running of the famed Santa Anita Maturity classic. Nine colts will compete for the richest prize ever offered for this event. The purse is in excess of $200,000. The distance is one and one fourth mile. The record is two minutes

222

flat. Now here comes Trafalgar in number one position, with Bob Willis up. Number two is Blazing High, Pete Hernandez up. Number three is Don't Bother Me, Johnny Johns in the irons. Number four is Victorio, with Ponce up. Number . . ."

The uproar in the stands drowned out the voice, and Ponce was snapped out of his trance by Victorio's violent lunge. The gray went up on his hind legs, came down and turned completely around. The bat in Ponce's hand popped against the crouching rump, and the mountain stallion steadied. He followed number three entry as if competing in a parade class at a horse show. Massive neck bowed, tiny ears pointed straight ahead, tail streaming like a silver flag, he danced along with that sliding, hesitating action.

At the end of the parade, the nine entries wheeled out of line and went up the track for the final loosening-up exercises. Ponce saw Bob Willis swinging across the track toward him as they rounded the clubhouse turn and he started down the backstretch at a slow canter. He tried to grin, only to find that his face was frozen stiff. He nodded then, and ran his glance over Trafalgar.

The lanky English racer moved with his usual violence, trying to grab the bit in his cold jaws. His long shoulders were wet, but no lather had yet appeared on his dark coat. Fractious he might be, but he was not a horse to leave his race in the stall.* Taking in the size of him and the long, wiry muscles, Ponce experienced a sinking sensation in the pit of his stomach. This was the one Victorio would have to beat!

The trumpet shrilled its final call, and the nine racers quickened their pace and approached the starting gate, which had been pulled into position at the half-mile post, directly back of the far turn. As horse after horse went into the narrow stalls, the stands fell silent again, then loud cries broke out as

* A racer that sweats too freely and becomes overly excited before a race is said to "Leave his race in the stall" or "at the gate," meaning he has burned up his energy before the race. Such high-strung animals are seldom top runners.

Trafalgar reared and attempted to wheel away. At an order from the starter, two handlers dashed in and brought the brown down and urged him into number one stall.

There was no sound, except the soothing whispers of riders talking to their mounts, the occasional rattle of rear gates being bumped . . . then these ceased altogether. One endless moment in which nothing moved . . . and suddenly the crashing jangle of the bell and the announcer's shout:

"They're off!"

In a blinding, deafening hail of dust, sand, clumps of dirt and shrill cries of jockeys, nine Thoroughbreds broke as one. Running with that curious, climbing action typical of blooded racers reaching for their top stride, the nine thundered for the first turn.

The outside horses dropped back, as the leaders forged off the straightaway in a scrambling, jostling rush. An instant later, the homestretch was looming up, impossibly long and empty. In position number one, the rangy English colt clung to the rail like a leech, his body stretching out, his legs flashing faster with every stride. Close on his heels, the chestnut Blazing High was making a strong bid to go up front.

Victorio had broken with the leaders, but midway around the turn, he fell back and started to drift out, despite everything Ponce could do to hold him steady. Now he was running with the pack, six lengths behind Trafalgar and Blazing High . . . running strongly, but failing to close up.

In the stretch drive, Blazing High started to falter, then moved up under pressure to make a try for the rail before the clubhouse turn. He made a dazzling rush and was challenging Trafalgar at the turn.

And Victorio was holding stubbornly to his place on the outside of the field! He moved almost clumsily. Completely unnerved by the terrifying clanging of the bell and the inhuman cries of the jockeys and the crowd, he seemed unable to collect himself.

The loudspeaker began its monotonous drone:

"Nearing the half, it's Trafalgar in the lead by half a length. Blazing High is second, and Blue Nose is third. Now Trafalgar is into the turn and pulling away from Blazing High, and Blue Nose is going out and falling back. Around the turn, it's still Trafalgar by two lengths, Blazing High second, and Blue Nose folding. At the top of the stretch, it's Trafalgar pulling away from Blazing High—The field is bunched in the turn. Trafalgar is four lengths on top and turning it on! Ladies and gentlemen, that Englishman can *run!*

"Now taking the stretch, it's Victorio moving up on Don't Bother Me and going on. Victorio moves out to the outside rail and closes up on Blazing High. Blazing High is fading fast. He can't take what Trafalgar's thrown at him. Victorio has taken second place now. He's going in for the kill! Ladies and gentlemen—it looks like a *race!*

"At the half, it's still Trafalgar out in front by three lengths, but Victorio's closing fast. And there goes Victorio up on the outside! He's wavering out. He's giving his rider trouble. Now he's on the outside rail. And going into the far turn, it's Trafalgar by three lengths, Victorio in number two place, and Don't Bother Me leaving the field to take number three. He's making his move, but it's not good enough.

"In the far turn, Trafalgar has opened up another half length. He's on top by three and a half. Victorio is on the outside rail. And at the mile, Trafalgar is leading by four lengths!

"At the head of the stretch, it's Trafalgar by four lengths, Victorio second by three lengths, and Don't Bother Me is trying to open up again. He's coming in on Victorio, but Victorio starts to move out!

"In the stretch, it's Trafalgar by three lengths, Victorio by four, and Don't Bother Me by six. Now it's Trafalgar by a length and a half, Victorio by eight, and Don't Bother Me in third place. Victorio is closing fast. He's challenging Trafalgar

for the lead! He's out in front by a nose, by a neck, by half a length.

"Going for the wire, it's Victorio by two lengths, Trafalgar by eight, and Don't Bother Me by four. And now it's Victorio going away, and *gone!*"

For a full minute the uproar was like one continuous roll of thunder. It seemed to come down from the very skies, blotting out sight as well as all other sound. It followed Ponce as he took Victorio on into the turn and slowed him. It surged up again as the announcer called out the names of the winner and those who had placed and showed. It numbed Ponce and sent Victorio up onto his hind legs as eager hands reached up to pull them into the winner's circle.

From all sides questions were being flung at the still-faced rider on the gigantic gray.

"Did you know you equaled the record?"

No, he did not know that.

"Were you in doubt as to the outcome?"

No, he had not been.

"How does it feel to own a sensational racer like Victorio?"

It felt very good.

"Are you going to continue racing him?"

Yes, he thought he probably would.

"When will you retire him?"

When Victorio tells him it is time to do that.

"Are you taking him back east?"

He would probably do that.

And the inevitable question: "Which of your horses is the faster, Victorio or Desert Storm?"

Ponce realized that the microphone was suddenly in front of him, and that the tumult had died away completely. For one moment he hesitated, then:

"If that were known, they would not both be entered in the Santa Anita Handicap."

Further questions were halted and changed to cries of alarm as the batteries of flash bulbs exploded and Victorio reared, squealing in terror. No one had prepared him for *that!* Biting his lips to keep from laughing outright, Ponce struck his mount on his right shoulder and wheeled him out of the closely packed square called the Winner's Circle. He glimpsed people spilling over the fence and starting toward him, and at that he banged his heels against Victorio's lathered ribs and put him into the chute at a canter.

Victorio had *run* for them! Did they want to *eat* him now? Glancing neither to right nor to left, he cantered on around the Seabiscuit Memorial, the George Woolf Memorial and the saddling paddock. Not until he entered the barn area did he pull Victorio to a walk. And not until he came in sight of Barn 99 and saw The Old Apache waiting in the fading sunlight before Victorio's stall did his face relax in a triumphant smile.

Twenty-six days raced past to the roaring clamor of the thousands of racing enthusiasts who daily packed the stands. Horses attained overnight fame . . . and faded from the picture forever. Through those days, Ponce was seldom absent from Barn 99. As each day ended, he mentally crossed it off and subtracted it from those still remaining. And when at last February 25 dawned, he still did not know which of his two horses he hoped would win the great Santa Anita Handicap. He forced himself to quit thinking about it as he donned the white and crimson racing silks he had chosen to represent his two-horse stable. And Joe Marino, Desert Storm's rider in the coming contest, knew what was troubling his friend—and did not ask the question.

The day had been overcast, with rain threatening since noon. The rain did not descend; neither did the sun win through the banks of clouds. As the bugle shrilled out its call to post at regular intervals, Ponce sat on the edge of a bench in the jockey's building, his gaze fixed on the floor. On his left, Joe Marino, dressed in identical racing silks, as the second half of the double entry, was equally silent and tense. On his right, Bob Willis could think of nothing to say either. For over three hours they had held that strained, alert position, breaking it only occasionally to get up and take a turn about the crowded room.

"The horses are entering the saddling shed in preparation for the sixth race of the day, the famed Santa Anita Handicap."

The loudspeaker, blaring directly above Ponce's head, made him jump in spite of himself. He blushed suddenly and glanced sideways, then laughed outright upon seeing his two companions in a position identical with his own—half rising, half sitting. There was something he had to tell Joe. Any minute now, the loudspeaker would send them out to the paddock. It would be too late then.

"Joe," he said, trying to keep his voice steady, "you are in number two stall, and I am in number three. If you can, get Desert Storm on the rail quickly. She drifts out in the turns— very badly."

Bob Willis heard that and grinned widely. "And where," he asked, "do you think Trafalgar will be all that time?"

"Hangin' onto Desert Storm's tail," Joe Marino shot back, his eyes twinkling. "*If he's lucky, that is!*"

"Oho!" Willis replied. "You just . . ."

"Riders out!" came the call, effectively silencing him. A moment later, the magnified voice was saying, "Ladies and gentlemen, the riders are entering the paddock to claim their mounts for the sixth race."

In traditional, police-guarded single-file, eleven wiry figures in brilliant silks and gleaming boots stepped into view. With typical "visitor's luck," the English-born Trafalgar had again managed to draw post position. And to complete the ironic picture, Joe Marino wore the white "2" on its black card pinned to his right shoulder, while Ponce walked in third place.

Delgadito stood at Desert Storm's head, waiting to give Joe Marino a hand up. Gabe Stuart, looking every inch the successful horseman, was holding Victorio's bridle ring as Ponce walked up and stood waiting for the signal to mount.

"As trainer of your stable," Gabe said with a grin, "I'm supposed to tell you how to ride this here race, so I will. *Ride it to win*, you hear?"

Ponce tried to reply, but his throat was like sandpaper, and he could only nod and wink.

"Reins over!"

In response to the command, eleven pairs of reins were lifted and passed over eleven high heads.

"*Riders up!*"

Gabe stooped, extending his right hand. Ponce's left foot touched it, his right leg bent, straightened, and the next instant he was settling himself atop the tiny pad of leather and steel, his hands gathering in the soft leather reins. He waited until he saw Joe Marino turn Desert Storm toward the chute, then moved Victorio out on the filly's heels. Behind him, eight riders, some with ponies siding them to help control their mounts, wound around the paddock and plunged into the shadowy chute.

There was an interval of near-darkness, then, just as Trafalgar lunged onto the track and turned up past the towering tiers of the stands, the sun burst from behind the clouds. Into this blinding glare, Ponce rode Victorio. He kept his gaze fastened on Desert Storm's haunches, directly in front of him. He was dimly aware of the loudspeaker starting the seemingly endless introductions. Trafalgar and Bob Willis received resounding applause. The big brown had taken three large purses since his defeat in the Maturity. The applause gained volume as Desert Storm and Joe Marino were announced. With her white stockings gleaming like snow against her black coat, and her crimson hood matching the crimson silks of her rider, the big filly was a sight to bring the most listless spectator to his feet. With genuine joy, the crowd welcomed her back.

Just as the announcer said, "Victorio . . ." Ponce banged his heels against the gray's ribs and jerked on the reins, stifling the violent reaction of his mount before it could begin. And though he knew the crowd was applauding wildly, the young Apache heard nothing at all. Once again he was riding through a completely silent vacuum. Automatically, he turned Victorio and moved him up alongside Desert Storm for the warm-up. He did not even hear the second ovation accorded the gray and the black as they swept past the stands in perfect unison.

Inside the starting gate were the dying sounds of rumps banging against rear-gates, whispered commands and impatient champing of bits. They faded . . . stopped. No one breathed; no one moved his eyes from his mount's ears.

And then the world turned upside down as the bell jangled and the gates crashed open.

Victorio broke fast, took two surging leaps, then stumbled. Terrified, Ponce felt the great shoulders sinking under him.

He threw all his weight back in an effort to pull the gray up. He heard screams rocketing off to his right and felt sure that a horse had gone down . . . perhaps more than one. He glimpsed a black form shooting out on his left and knew that Joe Marino was getting Desert Storm to the rail. And then Victorio was starting to move like a thunderbolt after the flashing leaders.

Ponce weaved back, caught his balance and flung himself flat against the straining neck. Through the whipping silver mane, he glimpsed the rear hoofs of the leader, but it was not Desert Storm, and it was not the leader, after all. A groan was wrenched from him as he saw a brown streak going into the turn, a full length ahead of Desert Storm and four lengths ahead of Victorio's out-thrust head. He uncocked his whip and touched the churning shoulder below his right knee. A bay was coming up on that side, threatening to cut in ahead of him. The bay dropped back out of sight, as if running backwards, and Ponce gasped for breath. Victorio had obeyed the demand for more speed with breathtaking suddenness and power. His dark legs were stretching farther with every stride, and at the top of the home stretch he was going strongly, less than half a length behind the madly running Desert Storm.

Victorio's move had taken him up in time to hold the filly from going out in the turn, and together they swept past the stands after the thundering Trafalgar. One glance was enough to show Ponce that the English colt was out to take this race. Held to the rail by Bob Willis and feeling the sting of the bat at every lengthening jump, he was setting a pace calculated to kill off all opposition in the opening sprint. He was displaying more power than Ponce had believed him capable of. His lead over Desert Storm and Victorio was increasing steadily.

Four lengths separated the leader from the black and the gray as the clubhouse turn rolled toward them, then tipped under them. It stretched to five as Desert Storm drifted out halfway around and crowded Victorio into the middle of the track. Then it ceased to widen.

Joe Marino's bat popped once against the thrusting, heaving shoulders of the filly, and she straightened immediately. The next instant, she was stretched out in a murderous drive. Like a comet, she bore down on the strongly running Trafalgar. At the half, she was within a nose of the bulging brown rump.

Caught completely off guard by the filly's blinding burst of speed, Ponce could not collect his wits until it was too late. He pulled himself out of the saddle and screamed into Victorio's flattened ears, and his right arm commenced to rise and fall with a steady rhythm. The thought flashed through his mind that, by giving his filly a helping hand in the clubhouse turn, he had unwittingly lost Victorio his opportunity to win the race!

Under the bat, Victorio lunged wildly, then began to reach out in those incredibly long strides. Within a hundred feet, he was fully extended, running with a curiously long, floating action. The action of a strider! Without quickening the tempo of his strides, he had his crimson hood at the tip of Desert Storm's tail as the filly went with Trafalgar into the far turn.

Ponce knew what would happen if he permitted Victorio to go on. In the instant before Desert Storm wavered, he pulled the rigid head of his mount to the left and took him up on the inside. Without looking, he knew that Desert Storm was running wide in the turn. . . . She had never been able to cling to the rail. And then light appeared between the rail and the streaking brown.

Trafalgar was going wide also!

In a flash, Ponce had Victorio's nose pointed at that slowly widening patch of light, and he was driving the gray into it with whip, hands and heels. He saw Bob Willis throw one startled look back and take Trafalgar out to allow Victorio running room. Pulled out, the brown wavered, then surged forward under the punishing whip as the track straightened.

Victorio was moving up with deadly intent, giving his all in the final drive. Feeling the awful strain in the body under him, Ponce knew the utter futility of demanding more speed. With his brain locked on the single thought, Victorio would give until he had nothing more in him to give.

Ponce turned the bat loose and let it dangle from its loop on his wrist.

Close to the rail, Victorio was flashing out to catch Trafalgar —and succeeding! His crimson hood edged up, inch by inch, drew even with Bob Willis' wildly working left foot and passed it. And then the crowd went mad as Desert Storm began moving in.

She came on . . . on . . . on . . . running madly, beautifully. Halfway down the stretch, she caught Trafalgar and matched him stride for stride. In the closing seconds of that heart-breaking struggle down the endless sweep of track, Joe Marino quit using the whip. Clearly, all too clearly, the magnificent filly was giving everything she had in an effort to hold on. No one could demand more.

And Victorio was leading by a head—only for an instant, though. A hundred feet from the wire, he faltered ever so slightly, and again three flaring, foam-matted muzzles were held straight by an invisible, ungiving wire.

The wire snapped.

Desert Storm dragged one final ounce of strength from somewhere deep inside her valiant heart and thrust her nose past Trafalgar's. The brown sprinter did not have what it took. He could not meet her challenge.

Victorio could!

He seemed to gather himself in mid-stride. In one uncoiling movement, he shot out to place his red-rimmed nostrils against the invisible barrier that once again stretched across the track. Head and head, nose and nose and stride for stride, the gray and the black streaked across the finish line.

"Photo finish!"

The letters blinked atop the tote boards. A moment later the announcer was telling the hysterical crowd that there would be a short delay until the films were developed.

Turning back toward the judges' stand, Ponce and Joe Marino exchanged brief, knowing glances. They did not have to wait for pictures to tell them the winner of the great struggle. They knew. They smiled tightly, in the way of men made uncomfortable by knowledge of greatness accomplished, as they came down the track. Horses, riders and handlers were dashing about in the purposeful disorder which is the aftermath of every race. Joe Marino took Desert Storm wide as Blue Nose reared nervously, throwing his rider, who was in the act of dismounting. Ponce, on his part, whirled Victorio away to avoid a collision with Trafalgar. The beaten brown was completely undone and he reared repeatedly, attempting to free himself of the two handlers who clung to his bridle and maneuvered him toward the chute.

The track was cleared at last. Only two horses remained, a gigantic gray that lunged about with increasing anger and fear and a powerful black that moved restlessly after the gray. They were unstrung by the deafening clamor raining down from the packed tiers. Again and again, they reared and tried to bolt up the track, to escape the terrifying confusion, but always they came down and continued their uneasy circling back and forth before the judges' stand.

"*Ladies and gentlemen!*" roared the loudspeaker. Silence fell instantly over the stand and field, as thousands strained to hear the fateful words. "The Santa Anita Handicap ended in a dead heat, with Desert Storm and Victorio taking first place. That's number two and three, ladies and gentlemen. Trafalgar finished in second place, Don't Bother Me finished third, and Blue Nose was fourth. The results of the race have been declared official."

That was all, so far as the spectators were concerned. The uproar surged out louder and louder, and a solid wave of humanity rolled toward the winner's circle. A cordon of policemen was thrown about the flower- and shrub-enclosed arena and a lane was opened to admit the two lathered winners.

Ponce glanced up and saw Joe Marino's eyes on him, bright and twinkling. The veteran jockey winked broadly and flashed him a smile, as if to offer him moral support during these trying moments. He started slightly when the cameras began flashing blindingly on all sides, then put all his attention into the business of keeping the enraged and terrified Victorio under control. He felt the great animal sinking away under him and struck the wet shoulders a sharp blow with the whip. The action came barely in time to prevent the gray from lunging straight into the sea of faces before him. Without warning, Victorio lashed out with both hind feet, almost unseating his rider, and again the whip slapped smartly. Ponce knew he could control the mountain stallion but a short time longer, knew he must dismount and get him away from there before something really serious occurred. He turned to ask Joe Marino when they could get down, only to find the jockey gone. Wildly he glanced about, feeling utterly deserted amid the confusion. A dozen reporters were trying to ask him questions at the same time, but he could make no sense from their remarks. An instant later, he heard Joe Marino's voice. Amplified and deepened by the loudspeaker, it did not sound like his friend's, but another voice kept calling him "Joe," so Ponce knew it must indeed be he. With a silencing gesture toward the impatient reporters, he kicked his feet free of the irons and slid to the ground. He was dimly aware that Delgadito was already at Victorio's head, dimly aware of Gabe Stuart holding Desert Storm's reins, a dozen feet away. Then Joe Marino's unfamiliar voice was coming from the loudspeaker again.

"No, I didn't know I had the race sewed up," the wiry rider said in evident denial of the announcer's suggestion. "I didn't know anything for sure, except that I had a terrific filly under me."

"Did you think Desert Storm could beat Trafalgar, Joe?" the announcer asked.

"I didn't *think* any such thing," came Joe's instant reply. "I *knew* she could." He paused, while a roar of laughter went up from the listeners, then stated with wry humor, "The only thing I got to wondering about was if there was going to be enough track left for her to do it in!"

"Did she give you any trouble?"

"In the turns," the jockey admitted honestly. "She's got a bad habit of lugging out, but that's her *only* fault."

"What about Victorio?" the announcer wanted to know. "When did you feel you had *him*?"

"You kiddin'?" the rider shot back. He made a face, enjoying this moment hugely, then said in that humorous way of his, "I knew I had him the second the announcer said, 'dead heat' and not one second before!"

Again laughter swelled out, and then hands were clutching Ponce's arms and dragging him toward the place where Joe Marino stood beside the announcer.

"What was your impression of the race, Ponce?" the man demanded. "Just when did you know you had the race in your pocket?"

Ponce frowned. "I did not *know* I had it," he stated quietly. "At the head of the stretch, I *thought* Victorio would go on up, but I did not *know*."

"Did Desert Storm's move surprise you?"

"Yes," Ponce admitted, nodding slowly. "Yes, that surprised me."

The announcer's next question was the one Ponce had been dreading, the one he had known would certainly come.

"You own the two winners, right?" He waited for Ponce's nod, then continued, "Which, in your opinion, is the faster and greater of the two, Desert Storm or Victorio?"

Ponce waited a long moment, the while he searched for the right answer to give the countless thousands who watched and listened. Quite honestly, then, he said, "I do not know the answer to that. I do not know, either, how Desert Storm managed to catch Victorio in this race. I think, though, she could not have gone past him."

There was a short pause. Suddenly a man stepped up to the announcer and whispered something in his ear. He was watching Ponce as he talked, and he went on watching him when he ceased and stood waiting for the announcer to speak.

"What would you say," the announcer asked excitedly, "if you were asked to match your two horses, one against the other?"

Ponce was too stunned to reply immediately. He caught his breath, swallowed and blinked rapidly. "You mean a match race?" he asked slowly.

"Exactly!"

"I had never thought of that. I think you must give me a little time. If it is what they want," he half turned and gestured toward the sea of faces, "it may be that Desert Storm and Victorio should run together again for them." He hesitated, than said again, "You must give me a little time."

The other would have pressed him for a definite answer then, but Ponce was finished. He turned and made his way through the close-pressed throng to where Delgadito and Gabe Stuart stood with the pair of horses that had this day proved their greatness to the world. He turned when someone shouted, "Give us a shot of you with your two winners, Ponce!"

Obediently, he took the reins from Gabe and Delgadito and stood between the two huge animals. For a moment he felt very small . . . and completely alone, but when the cameras had clicked once and for all, he turned to look at his racers. Instantly, his own uneasiness vanished as his eyes read the almost senseless terror which possessed Desert Storm and Victorio. He sent his voice into their ears, speaking steadily in

the Apache tongue they had come to know. Gradually, the tension left them. The filly reached out to nuzzle his gleaming silks, and the stallion, true to his nature, attempted to sample the same silken material with his teeth, until Ponce spoke firmly to him.

"Desert Storm," he murmured, "and Victorio—the victorious one. So they shout when they see you run, like the winds from the desert and the mountains. I have a thought. You should have one name between you, for what you have done this day. 'Los Victorios,' the victorious ones, for so you are to me. *Enju.* It is well, is it not?"

PRONUNCIATION AND EXPLANATION
REFERENCE

BACKSTRETCH——Usually referred to simply as "the stretch." The straight stretch of track on the far side directly following the clubhouse turn.

BAT——A slender whip with a loop or a series of small leather strips affixed to the end.

BOWED TENDON——A much-dreaded injury to a horse's front legs. The big tendon pulls loose from the bone, resulting in the tendon's assuming the shape of a strung bow.

BRONCO——A term applied to an unbroken wild horse.

BRUSH——Another term for bat or whip.

CLUBHOUSE TURN——The turn in the track on the grandstand's right.

DALLO CHIE——(dah-yo-chee) An Apache word meaning "Son of the Roper."

DELGADITO——(del-gah-deeto) Spanish for "The slender one."

DRIVE——A term signifying that a horse is moving under pressure from his rider. A straining effort to increase speed and maintain it over a distance.

EARLY-FOOT——The ability of a horse to "scat" or break from the starting gate at top speed.

EQUIPOISE——(eh-kwi-poyz) A latin word meaning "Of Perfect Balance." Also the name of one of the all-time greats of the track.

FAR TURN——The turn to the left of the grandstands.

HAGAR——(hay-gar) An ancient Hebrew word meaning "Flight."

HANDICAP——A term indicating the equalizing process whereby various entries are assigned weights (lead tabs) according to sex, age, number of wins, etc. The addition of so much as a mere pound often spells the difference between victory and defeat.

HOME STRETCH——Usually referred to simply as "The Lane" or "Home Lane." It is the straight stretch directly in front of the stands.

HOOD or BLINKERS——A covering for a horse's head, usually of light canvas or felt, equipped with cup-like attachments behind the eyes to prevent the horse from being distracted.

INDIAN BRIDLE——A halter fashioned with a slip noose over the nostrils to control unmanageable animals.

ISHMAEL——(ish-may-el) An ancient Hebrew word meaning "Wanderer."

JOCKEYS' BUILDING——The building or room in which riders dress and wait between races. It is guarded at all times and only grooms and racing officials are permitted to speak with the riders between races.

JOTO——(ho-to) An Apache word meaning "One-eyed giant."

JUAN——(hwan) John

LUG——A term indicating a horse's tendency to run counter to guidance, i.e. "lug in" toward the rail, or "lug out" toward the outside.

MUSTANERO——(moos-tan-yaro) The name given to a little-known group of wild horse runners in the southern and southwestern section of the U. S. and northern Mexico.

MUSTANG——A species of wild horse formerly found in the southwestern part of the U. S.

PONCE——(pon-say) Meaning "leap" or "jump."

RATE——To govern a horse's speed.

REATA——A slender rope of braided rawhide or horsehair, commonly used in the southwest.

RECEIVING BARN——The building holding the offices of track officials, veterinarians, etc. All horses must report to this building to be examined, stabled and checked into the grounds.

ROUTER——A distance horse as opposed to a sprinter.

SADDLING PADDOCK——(or shed) The place where the horses are saddled for a race. Usually located to one side of the stands or behind them, it is occasionally situated directly in front of the stands so that the crowds may observe the ritual.

SPRINT——A term signifying a horse's running at top speed, usually over a short distance, as opposed to a drive.

STOCKINGS——Wrappings of linen or other stout material used for wrapping horses' legs. Sometimes applied to support a real or suspected weakness, they are also employed in doctoring various ailments of the legs.

TRAFALGAR——(tra-fal-gar) The name of the famous square in London named in honor of Lord Nelson's victory over Napoleon's fleet.

TOTE BOARD——Officially known as the "Teetotalizing machine," it is a large board equipped with lighted numbers indicating the betting odds on each race and is situated in the infield directly across from the stands.

VICTORIO——(vik-tor-eeo) Spanish for "The Victorious One."

WINNER'S CIRCLE——An enclosure in front of the stands into which the winner of a race is led for the awarding of trophies, prizes, etc. Despite its name, it is more frequently square or rectangular in shape than circular.

YOSEN——(yoh-sen) The Apache Supreme Being, commonly translated as "Giver of Life."

LOGAN FORSTER

says of himself: "I have done a little of everything. I served six years as Pharmacist's Mate in the Navy, bucked and felled timber in Oregon, worked in lumber mills, ploughed wheatland in Texas, attended the University of Colorado and served as director for The Nomad Players in Boulder, Colorado. A few years ago, I withdrew from school to brave the "writing world." My DESERT STORM books are part of the result.

"My hobbies range from playing the piano through working with charcoals and pastels—to horses. From whatever angle you look at me, you'll see HORSES in the background, because they comprise the major part of my life. I am still in quest of that Arizona ranch, and as soon as I find it, I'll move my horses onto it and go wild with them!

"I am never happier than when working with my horses, unless it be when I am writing about them. As a matter of fact, it was while I was battling my own young Arabian stallion, one day, that I decided to write a story about the training of a stallion. THE MOUNTAIN STALLION is the result of a certain tussle which ended with me on the stable floor and Mighwar on top of me— and all because I was trying to inject some medicine into his infected right foreleg!

"Whenever I cannot be found around my own horses, I can be found at the race track—just *any* race track! In my estimation, there is no thrill in the world equal to that experienced by a lover of horses when a field of great Thoroughbreds thunders past the judge's stand in that mad, flying scramble for the lead and the rail. To me, the great striders seem always to be just on the verge of taking off into the air during that first driving sprint. And for me, life's one great question is answered each time I see 'The Fast Ones' run. Why am I running? I am running because I want to win! I think I can beat all the rest—if not this time, then surely the next—or the next. And if I lose, it won't be for lack of trying!"

Lightning Source UK Ltd.
Milton Keynes UK
UKOW011555250712

196561UK00006B/17/P